THE HISTORY & CULTURE of NATIVE AMERICANS

The

Navajo

THE HISTORY & CULTURE
of NATIVE AMERICANS

THE HISTORY & CULTURE
of NATIVE AMERICANS

The
Navajo

JENNIFER DENETDALE

Series Editor
PAUL C. ROSIER

CHELSEA HOUSE
An Infobase Learning Company

The Navajo

Chelsea House
An imprint of Infobase Learning
132 West 31st Street
New York NY 10001

Library of Congress Cataloging-in-Publication Data
Denetdale, Jennifer.
  The Navajo / by Jennifer Denetdale.
    p. cm. — (The history and culture of Native Americans)
  Includes bibliographical references and index.
  ISBN 978-1-60413-792-7 (hardcover)
  1. Navajo Indians–History. 2. Navajo Indians--Government relations. 3. Navajo Indians--Social life and customs. I. Title. II. Series.

  E99.N3D368 2011
  979.1004'9726--dc22   2011007223

Chelsea House books are available at special discounts when purchased in bulk quantities for businesses, associations, institutions, or sales promotions. Please call our Special Sales Department in New York at (212) 967-8800 or (800) 322-8755.'

You can find Chelsea House on the World Wide Web at
http://www.infobaselearning.com

Text design by Lina Farinella
Cover design by Alicia Post
Composition by Julie Adams
Cover printed by Yurchak Printing, Landisville, Pa.
Book printed and bound by Yurchak Printing, Landisville, Pa.
Date printed: July 2011
Printed in the United States of America

10 9 8 7 6 5 4 3 2 1
This book is printed on acid-free paper.

All links and Web addresses were checked and verified to be correct at the time of publication. Because of the dynamic nature of the Web, some addresses and links may have changed since publication and may no longer be valid.

Contents

Foreword
by Paul C. Rosier

Native American words, phrases, and tribal names are embedded in the very geography of the United States—in the names of creeks, rivers, lakes, cities, and states, including Alabama, Connecticut, Iowa, Kansas, Illinois, Missouri, Oklahoma, and many others. Yet Native Americans remain the most misunderstood ethnic group in the United States. This is a result of limited coverage of Native American history in middle schools, high schools, and colleges; poor coverage of contemporary Native American issues in the news media; and stereotypes created by Hollywood movies, sporting events, and TV shows.

Two newspaper articles about American Indians caught my eye in recent months. Paired together, they provide us with a good introduction to the experiences of American Indians today: first, how they are stereotyped and turned into commodities; and second, how they see themselves being a part of the United States and of the wider world. (Note: I use the terms *Native Americans* and *American Indians* interchangeably; both terms are considered appropriate.)

In the first article, "Humorous Souvenirs to Some, Offensive Stereotypes to Others," written by Carol Berry in *Indian Country Today*, I read that tourist shops in Colorado were selling "souvenir" T-shirts portraying American Indians as drunks. "My Indian name is Runs with Beer," read one T-shirt offered in Denver. According to the article, the T-shirts are "the kind of stereotype-reinforcing products also seen in nearby Boulder, Estes Park, and likely other Colorado communities, whether as part of the tourism trade or as everyday merchandise." No other ethnic group in the United States is stereotyped in such a public fashion. In addition, Native people are used to sell a range of consumer goods, including the Jeep Cherokee, Red Man chewing tobacco, Land O'Lakes butter, and other items that either objectify or insult them, such as cigar store Indians. As importantly, non-Indians learn about American Indian history and culture through sports teams such as the Atlanta Braves, Cleveland Indians, Florida State Seminoles, or Washington Redskins, whose name many American Indians consider a racist insult; dictionaries define *redskin* as a "disparaging" or "offensive" term for American Indians. When fans in Atlanta do their "tomahawk chant" at Braves baseball games, they perform two inappropriate and related acts: One, they perpetuate a stereotype of American Indians as violent; and two, they tell a historical narrative that covers up the violent ways that Georgians treated the Cherokee during the Removal period of the 1830s.

The second article, written by Melissa Pinion-Whitt of the San Bernardino *Sun* addressed an important but unknown dimension of Native American societies that runs counter to the irresponsible and violent image created by products and sporting events. The article, "San Manuels Donate $1.7 M for Aid to Haiti," described a Native American community that had sent aid to Haiti after it was devastated in January 2010 by an earthquake that killed more than 200,000 people, injured hundreds of thousands more, and destroyed the Haitian capital. The San Manuel Band of Mission Indians in California donated $1.7 million to help relief efforts in Haiti; San Manuel children held fund-raisers to collect additional donations. For the San Manuel Indians it was nothing new; in 2007 they had donated $1 million to help Sudanese refugees in Darfur. San Manuel also contributed $700,000 to relief efforts following Hurricane Katrina and Hurricane Rita, and donated $1 million in 2007 for wildfire recovery in Southern California.

Such generosity is consistent with many American Indian nations' cultural practices, such as the "give-away," in which wealthy tribal members give to the needy, and the "potlatch," a winter gift-giving ceremony and feast tradition shared by tribes in the Pacific

Northwest. And it is consistent with historical accounts of American Indians' generosity. For example, in 1847 Cherokee and Choctaw, who had recently survived their forced march on a "Trail of Tears" from their homelands in the American South to present-day Oklahoma, sent aid to Irish families after reading of the potato famine, which created a similar forced migration of Irish. A Cherokee newspaper editorial, quoted in Christine Kinealy's *The Great Irish Famine: Impact, Ideology, and Rebellion*, explained that the Cherokee "will be richly repaid by the consciousness of having done a good act, by the moral effect it will produce abroad." During and after World War II, nine Pueblo communities in New Mexico offered to donate food to the hungry in Europe, after Pueblo army veterans told stories of suffering they had witnessed while serving in the United States armed forces overseas. Considering themselves a part of the wider world, Native people have reached beyond their borders, despite their own material poverty, to help create a peaceful world community.

American Indian nations have demonstrated such generosity within the United States, especially in recent years. After the terrorist attacks of September 11, 2001, the Lakota Sioux in South Dakota offered police officers and emergency medical personnel to New York City to help with relief efforts; Indian nations across the country sent millions of dollars to help the victims of the attacks. As an editorial in the *Native American Times* newspaper explained on September 12, 2001, "American Indians love this country like no other. . . . Today, we are all New Yorkers."

Indeed, Native Americans have sacrificed their lives in defending the United States from its enemies in order to maintain their right to be both American and Indian. As the volumes in this series tell us, Native Americans patriotically served as soldiers (including as "code talkers") during World War I and World War II, as well as during the Korean War, the Vietnam War, and, after 9/11, the wars in Afghanistan and Iraq. Native soldiers, men and women, do so today by the tens of thousands because they believe in America, an America that celebrates different cultures and peoples. Sgt. Leonard Gouge, a Muscogee Creek, explained it best in an article in *Cherokee News Path* in discussing his post-9/11 army service. He said he was willing to serve his country abroad because "by supporting the American way of life, I am preserving the Indian way of life."

This new Chelsea House series has two main goals. The first is to document the rich diversity of American Indian societies and the ways their cultural practices and traditions have evolved over time. The second goal is to provide the reader with coverage of the complex relationships that have developed between non-Indians and Indians over the past several hundred years. This history helps to explain why American Indians consider themselves both American and Indian and why they see preserving this identity as a strength of the American way of life, as evidence to the rest of the world that America is a champion of cultural diversity and religious freedom. By exploring Native Americans' cultural diversity and their contributions to the making of the United States, these volumes confront the stereotypes that paint all American Indians as the same and portray them as violent; as "drunks," as those Colorado T-shirts do; or as rich casino owners, as many news accounts do.

* * *

Each of the 14 volumes in this series is written by a scholar who shares my conviction that young adult readers are both fascinated by Native American history and culture and have not been provided with sufficient material to properly understand the diverse nature of this complex history and culture. The authors themselves represent a varied group that includes university teachers and professional writers, men and women, and Native and non-Native. To tell these fascinating stories, this talented group of scholars has examined an incredible variety of sources, both the primary sources that historical actors have created and the secondary sources that historians and anthropologists have written to make sense of the past.

Although the 14 Indian nations (also called tribes and communities) selected for this series have different histories and cultures, they all share certain common experiences. In particular, they had to face an American empire that spread westward in the eighteenth and nineteenth centuries, causing great trauma and change for all Native people in the process. Because each volume documents American Indians' experiences dealing with powerful non-Indian institutions and ideas, I outline below the major periods and features of federal Indian policy-making in order to provide a frame of reference for complex processes of change with which American Indians had to contend. These periods—Assimilation, Indian New Deal, Termination, Red Power, and Self-determination—and specific acts of legislation that define them—in particular the General Allotment Act, the Indian Reorganization Act, and the Indian Self-determination and Education Assistance Act—will appear in all the volumes, especially in the latter chapters.

In 1851, the commissioner of the federal Bureau of Indian Affairs (BIA) outlined a three-part program for subduing American Indians militarily and assimilating them into the United States: concentration, domestication, and incorporation. In the first phase, the federal government waged war with the American Indian nations of the American West in order to "concentrate" them on reservations, away from expanding settlements of white Americans and immigrants. Some American Indian nations experienced terrible violence in resisting federal troops and state militia; others submitted peacefully and accepted life on a reservation. During this phase, roughly from the 1850s to the 1880s, the U.S. government signed hundreds of treaties with defeated American Indian nations. These treaties "reserved" to these American Indian nations specific territory as well as the use of natural resources. And they provided funding for the next phase of "domestication."

During the domestication phase, roughly the 1870s to the early 1900s, federal officials sought to remake American Indians in the mold of white Americans. Through the Civilization Program, which actually started with President Thomas Jefferson, federal officials sent religious missionaries, farm instructors, and teachers to the newly created reservations in an effort to "kill the Indian to save the man," to use a phrase of that time. The ultimate goal was to extinguish American Indian cultural traditions and turn American Indians into Christian yeoman farmers. The most important piece of legislation in this period was the General Allotment Act (or Dawes Act), which mandated that American Indian nations sell much of their territory to white farmers and use the proceeds to farm on what was left of their homelands. The program was a failure, for the most part, because white farmers got much of the best arable land in the process. Another important part of the domestication agenda was the federal boarding school program, which required all American Indian children to attend schools to further their rejection of Indian ways and the adoption of non-Indian ways. The goal of federal reformers, in sum, was to incorporate (or assimilate) American Indians into American society as individual citizens and not as groups with special traditions and religious practices.

During the 1930s some federal officials came to believe that American Indians deserved the right to practice their own religion and sustain their identity as Indians, arguing that such diversity made America stronger. During the Indian New Deal period of the 1930s, BIA commissioner John Collier devised the Indian Reorganization Act (IRA), which passed in 1934, to give American Indian nations more power, not less. Not all American Indians supported the IRA, but most did. They were eager to improve their reservations, which suffered from tremendous poverty that resulted in large measure from federal policies such as the General Allotment Act.

Some federal officials opposed the IRA, however, and pushed for the assimilation of American Indians in a movement called Termination. The two main goals of Termination advocates, during the 1950s and 1960s, were to end (terminate) the federal reservation system and American Indians' political sovereignty derived from treaties and to relocate American Indians from rural reservations to urban areas. These coercive federal assimilation policies in turn generated resistance from Native Americans, including young activists who helped to create the so-called Red Power era of the 1960s and 1970s, which coincided with the African-American civil rights movement. This resistance led to the federal government's rejection of Termination policies in 1970. And in 1975 the U.S. Congress passed the Indian Self-determination and Education Assistance Act, which made it the government's policy to support American Indians' right to determine the future of their communities. Congress then passed legislation to help American Indian nations to improve reservation life; these acts strengthened American Indians' religious freedom, political sovereignty, and economic opportunity.

All American Indians, especially those in the western United States, were affected in some way by the various federal policies described above. But it is important to highlight the fact that each American Indian community responded in different ways to these pressures for change, both the detribalization policies of assimilation and the retribalization policies of self-determination. There is no one group of "Indians." American Indians were and still are a very diverse group. Some embraced the assimilation programs of the federal government and rejected the old traditions; others refused to adopt non-Indian customs or did so selectively, on their own terms. Most American Indians, as I noted above, maintain a dual identity of American and Indian.

Today, there are more than 550 American Indian (and Alaska Natives) nations recognized by the federal government. They have a legal and political status similar to states, but they have special rights and privileges that are the result of congressional acts and the hundreds of treaties that still govern federal-Indian relations today. In July 2008, the total population of American Indians (and Alaska Natives) was 4.9 million, representing about 1.6 percent of the United States population. The state with the highest number of American Indians is California, followed by Oklahoma, home to the Cherokee (the largest American Indian nation in terms of population), and then Arizona, home to the Navajo (the second-largest American Indian nation). All told, roughly half of the American Indian population lives in urban areas; the other half lives on reservations and in other rural parts of the country. Like all their fellow American citizens, American Indians pay federal taxes, obey federal laws, and vote in federal, state, and local elections; they also participate in the democratic processes of their American Indian nations, electing judges, politicians, and other civic officials.

This series on the history and culture of Native Americans celebrates their diversity and differences as well as the ways they have strengthened the broader community of America. Ronnie Lupe, the chairman of the White Mountain Apache government in Arizona, once addressed questions from non-Indians as to "why Indians serve the United States with such distinction and honor?" Lupe, a Korean War veteran, answered those questions during the Gulf War of 1991–1992, in which Native American soldiers served to protect the independence of the Kuwaiti people. He explained in "Chairman's Corner" in the *Fort Apache Scout* that "our loyalty to the United States goes beyond our need to defend our home and reservation lands. . . . Only a few in this country really understand that the indigenous people are a national treasure. Our values have the potential of creating the social, environmental, and spiritual healing that could make this country truly great."

—Paul C. Rosier
Associate Professor of History
Villanova University

The Navajo Nation and Its People

On New Year's Eve in 2009, Diné (or Navajo as they are better known in the American mainstream) arrived at the Navajo Nation Museum in Window Rock, Arizona, for a traditional winter game of Késhjéé', or the Shoe Game. Based upon a traditional story about how day and night were determined when the world was being created, the Shoe Game is played in the winter, usually when a ceremony is taking place. Today the betting game is played in homes and at gathering places such as chapter houses or the museum. In the early hours of the new year, the winning teams took home prizes like truckloads of firewood and an assortment of foodstuffs like Blue Bird flour, baking powder, sugar, salt, and coffee. The playing of the Shoe Game in a modern complex of the Navajo Nation's capital reflects how traditional cultural practices exist alongside modern Navajo life.

Indeed, many Navajo referred to the narratives associated with traditional gambling games when they discussed the possibility of the Navajo Nation entering the gaming business. Despite strong opposition from many Navajo, the Navajo Nation officially opened the Fire Rock casino near Gallup, New Mexico, in 2008. In 2010, the Navajo Nation opened a second casino on its northeastern border at Hogback, New Mexico, and it has plans to open up two more casinos. Navajo leaders are encouraged by the success of the Fire Rock casino and are optimistic that the planned casinos will prove equally profitable.

A six-year-old girl participates in a traditional Navajo Shoe Game in Arizona. She is looking for a buried shoe in which a ball of yucca stem is hidden.

The Treaty of 1868, signed between Navajo leaders and American officials, formally recognized a Navajo land base and the sovereign status of the Navajo Nation and its people. Although the treaty affirmed Navajo land holdings, it acknowledged only a fraction of what the Navajo considered their aboriginal territory. In the decades following the treaty, the Navajo land base was increased through presidential executive orders and congressional acts. The Navajo land base includes regions of Arizona, New Mexico, and Utah. Today, the Navajo Nation has a land base of nearly 18 million acres (7.2 million hectares) and includes three satellite communities: Alamo, Ramah, and To'hajiili, all in New Mexico. The Navajo Nation also owns the Big Boquillas ranch in western Arizona, which was purchased in 1987.

The 2000 census counted the Navajo population at 275,000, with about half living in urban areas beyond the borders of the Navajo Nation. The Navajo Nation follows a policy of enrolling as citizens those who can show proof of at least one-quarter Navajo blood. Other names that the Diné (which translates as "The People") call themselves are Náhookah Diné or "Earth Surface People," and Bilá 'ashdla', or "Five-Fingered Ones."

The Navajo homeland is a region of contrasts and varied vegetation, of towering mountains, steep cliffs, and flatlands. It is a place of pine trees in the higher elevations and scrub brush in the more arid flatlands. Some citizens live in communities that were created to provide federal and tribal government services to the Navajo people, including Window Rock, Chinle, Tuba City, and Shiprock. Still other Navajo live in rural areas in much the same manner as their grandparents and great-grandparents had lived, which often includes caring for livestock. For more than two centuries, the

(*Opposite*) This map shows the approximate location of major tribes in the Southwest Culture Area just before contact with Europeans. The Navajo land base now includes regions of Arizona, Mexico, and Utah.

Navajo have been a pastoral people who follow their herds of sheep and goats across the seasons in search of pasturage. Today, those values associated with livestock still shape Navajo society.

From the 1930s to the late 1940s, the federal government mandated the reduction of Navajo livestock because they were seen as the culprit of environmental devastation. The Navajo were to reduce their flocks by 50 percent. In the aftermath of

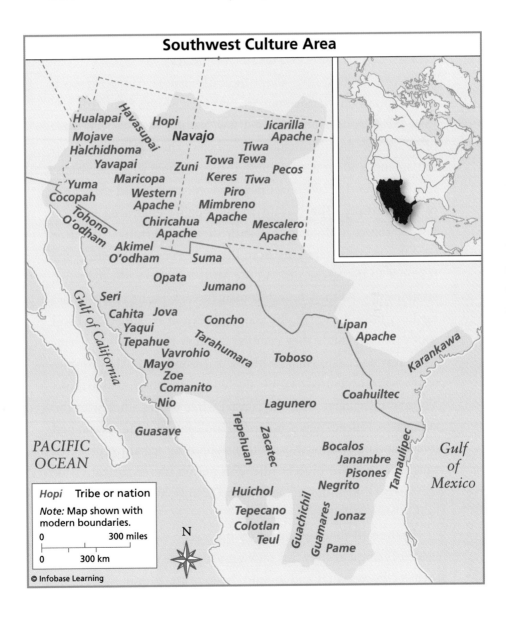

Southwest Culture Area

Hualapai
Havasupai
Hopi
Mojave
Navajo
Halchidhoma
Yavapai
Yuma
Cocopah
Maricopa
Tohono O'odham
Western Apache
Chiricahua Apache
Akimel O'odham
Jicarilla Apache
Tiwa
Towa Tewa
Zuni
Keres Tiwa
Piro
Mimbreno Apache
Pecos
Mescalero Apache
Suma
Opata
Jumano
Seri
Cahita Jova
Concho
Lipan Apache
Yaqui
Tepahue
Tarahumara
Vavrohio
Mayo
Toboso
Karankawa
Zoe
Comanito
Nio
Lagunero
Coahuiltec
Guasave
Tepehuan
Zacatec
Tamaulipec
PACIFIC OCEAN
Bocalos
Janambre
Pisones
Negrito
Gulf of Mexico
Gulf of California
Huichol
Guachichil
Guamares
Tepecano
Colotlan
Teul
Jonaz
Pame

Hopi Tribe or nation

Note: Map shown with modern boundaries.

0   300 miles
0   300 km

N

© Infobase Learning

the reduction, which destroyed Navajo reliance on livestock for subsistence, many Navajo migrated to urban areas in search of employment and education opportunities. Today, out of necessity, Navajo continue to cross the boundaries between Navajo land and urban areas, for the unemployment rate on the Nation hovers around 48 percent. The journeys back and forth across imaginary boundaries reflect strong attachments to cultural values that still shape their lives, no matter where they live.

INFLUENCE OF THE COLONIZERS

Much of what is known about the early history of the Navajo is based upon non-Navajo sources, and because the Spaniards and then the Mexicans encountered few Navajo, their reports were often second- and thirdhand. Nevertheless, these colonizers, their settlements, and the material culture they brought with them transformed the early Navajo in dramatic ways and shaped the course of their history. The Navajo so thoroughly embraced Spanish horses, sheep, and goats that their creation narratives describe how the animals were gifts from the Holy People, or deities. The presence of the Spaniards and the Mexicans also reshaped tribal relationships. As the Ute and Comanche were pushed into Navajo territory from the north, the ancestral Navajo expanded west and south into the lands they claimed through their creation narratives. Navajo relationships with the surrounding Pueblo peoples were also reconfigured as some Pueblo Indians continued to trade, ally, and intermarry with the Navajo while others allied with the colonizers. Indeed, new scholarship indicates that the Navajo had long-standing relationships with neighboring tribal peoples that ranged from peaceful to hostile. This period was so formative for the Navajo that anthropologist David Brugge has characterized it as the "Navajo cultural renaissance."

By the early nineteenth century, the Navajo had acquired a reputation of being a wealthy and autonomous people who had expanded their territory within and around the four sacred mountains. The largest political unit was a "natural community," which consisted of 10 to 20 extended families all related by clan and led by a headman. Navajo society was also matrilineal, meaning that a person's identity was rooted in the mother's clan; matrilineality shaped how all decisions were made. Women mattered, for they dictated land use, owned hogans (homes) and livestock, and made the decisions about children. Indeed, the textiles that women wove were an important trade item throughout the Southwest. In all layers of society, a philosophy called Hózhó guided life. According to Hózhó, Navajo continually seek good health, peace, and prosperity throughout their lives, with their kin relations, and the natural world.

However, in the course of American expansion from the mid-nineteenth century to the present, Navajo political, economic, religious, and social structures were transformed, so that today much of the Navajo way of life has been profoundly shaped and influenced by American assimilation practices. Today, these assimilation policies are considered ethnic cleansing. Ethnic cleansing refers to a state's intention to destroy all or part of a distinct group of people. Beginning with the military defeat of the Navajo in the mid-nineteenth century, traditional leaders saw their authority diminished as the United States claimed Navajo as their wards. By the 1920s, a federally dictated leadership was put in place. These leaders—the first tribal council—were expected to give approval for the development of gas and oil in the northern region of the Navajo reservation. That first council developed into the modern tribal government of the 1950s and '60s.

Fashioned under the Indian Reorganization Act of 1934, the modern Navajo government is organized under three branches: the executive, legislative, and judicial. Working with the president and vice president (executive branch), the 88-member tribal council (legislative branch) represents 110 chapters—the local political units around which communities are organized. In 2011, after much debate and controversy among the Navajo, the council was reduced to 24 members. The judicial branch includes the

Window Rock (*above*), located in Arizona, is capital of the Navajo Nation and the seat of the tribal government. Set up under the Indian Reorganization Act to mirror the U.S. government, the Navajo government has three branches: executive, legislative, and judicial.

Navajo Supreme Court, which addresses and interprets laws and legislation. Today, only the peacemaking court in the judicial unit is founded upon Navajo principles of justice. The peacemaking court addresses civil matters, like disputes over land use between families and clans, and acts as mediator between families and married couples. Presently, Navajo leaders are in the midst of government reform in which some are calling for a return to a government founded upon traditional principles.

As a modern nation, the Navajo face many challenges, including the imperative to become a fully sovereign nation with its own political, economic, and social structure separate from that of the United States. Navajo leaders strive to foster economic development, create jobs for their citizens, protect the land from ongoing environmental destruction, raise the education level of their people, and promote and preserve traditional cultural practices and the Diné language. Navajo history is about the creation and cultural evolution of the People, how they came to settle in the Southwest, and how they responded to centuries of foreign colonial invasions. Navajo people have a history similar to that of other indigenous peoples who steadfastly challenged and resisted American expansion into their homelands and the appropriation of their land, resources, and culture. For the Navajo, knowing one's history provides tools to address the present and the future, with all of its problems and promises. Many Navajo continue to cherish the age-old values that their ancestors lived by and so, this particular history is cognizant of the vitality of traditional teachings. Today, the Navajo face many challenges, many of which are direct consequences of American colonialism.

Navajo Origins and Early History

As a boy growing up in Fruitland, New Mexico, in the northeastern region of Navajoland, Frank Nez was apprenticed to his father, who was a Lightning Way singer. As a part of his education, he sat with his father on winter nights on the dirt floor of their hogan and listened to the creation narratives. As the nights unfolded, young Frank heard how the world began in the First World with First Man and First Woman, how Coyote was always subverting the natural order, how the boundaries of Diné Bekéyah (Navajo land) were established with mountain soil brought from the world below, and how the birth of Changing Woman was the dawn of a new age, a promise of beauty and harmony in the world. He heard about how the Twin Heroes earned the warrior's implements after they thwarted their father's attempts to destroy them, and how they then saved the people from monsters who roamed the earth.

In the 1930s and '40s, Navajo youth like Frank were still enmeshed in a traditional education based upon values within creation narratives and ceremonial knowledge. Like other youth of his age, he was accustomed to caring for the family's sheep, goats, and horses and helping with the fields where corn, beans, squash, and melons were planted. When he was about 10 years

Storytelling is an integral part of the Native American tradition. Young Navajo children are brought up listening to creation stories and other ceremonial knowledge.

old, he was sent to boarding schools, first at Ignacio, Colorado, and eventually to Stewart Indian School in Carson City, Nevada, where he was enrolled in the five-year program and trained as an automobile mechanic. After many years away, Frank returned to his homeland, but only after he had married a Navajo woman, Rose, whom he met at Stewart, and completed a tour with the U.S. Army during the Korean War.

By the time Navajo youth like Frank heard the traditional stories, the Navajo world had shifted from one based on livestock-raising to one in which the Navajo were forced to seek jobs because the livestock reduction program had devastated the economy. By the late 1940s, many Navajo left their homeland in search of jobs while children were forcibly sent to boarding schools. The impact of American expansion and federal Indian policies on the Navajo are reflected in Frank's life and in the ways that the Navajo strive to preserve traditional philosophies, practices, and ceremonial knowledge. Today, there are still young Navajo who are apprenticed to medicine people to learn the stories and the accompanying ceremonies, but for the most part, Navajo leaders, educators, and parents worry about the extent of language and cultural loss.

In the twenty-first century, the Navajo continue to rely on medicine people to restore and re-create balance and harmony through a number of healing, blessing, and protection ceremonies. Many are learning again about the sacredness of the Diné language and about traditional stories and practices through various venues, including contemporary songs, poetry, cultural performances, and modern storytelling. Some, like former Miss Navajo and now professional storyteller Sunny Dooley and Navajo cultural teacher Ernest Harry Begay, are routinely invited to regional and local schools and cultural events to share their knowledge of Navajo culture and history. They speak to packed rooms of educators, scholars, and parents who desire to keep the stories alive. Amazingly, these stories and ceremonies continue to be sources for Navajo identities, from the personal to the Nation.

This chapter offers some of the best-known traditional stories and gives examples of how they are the source for telling about the history and cultural practices of Navajo society. This chapter also explores how the Navajo claim the region between the four sacred mountains as their homeland, as well as how the ancestral Navajo were shaped by their contacts with neighboring tribes, such as the various Pueblo Indians, which resulted in their own population increase and the incorporation of a non-Navajo material culture to create a distinctively Navajo culture.

IN THE BEGINNING

All indigenous peoples in what is now the United States have their own stories of the origins of the universe and world and their places in those worlds. These narratives outline how they came to be humans and what their relationships are to the natural and human worlds. Importantly, these stories root Native peoples to the land. In the early twentieth century, anthropologist Gladys Reichard attempted to create a taxonomy (classification) of Navajo narratives and ceremonies, which was published as *Navaho Religion*. Her effort indicates that it is difficult to categorize and classify Navajo narratives and ceremonies in neat outlines. Rather, the narratives are performed as part of blessing, healing, and protection ceremonies and are manifested in a variety of ways. Today, the ways that the Navajo remember the traditional narratives include contemporary storytelling, cultural performances, poetry and prose, plays, and films.

The present world that the Navajo inhabit is the Glittering World, and depending on the version heard, it is the fourth or the fifth world. The progenitors (founders) of the Navajo journeyed through a series of worlds and emerged in a region called Dinétah, meaning the Navajo homeland. Dinétah is sacred geography, a place where many of the interactions between Holy Beings and other beings shaped the Navajo world. The people who became Navajo emerged into the Glittering World after a long and difficult

Navajo have a rich artistic history that has great meaning to the culture. Writing, storytelling, and performing arts help Navajo traditional
narratives endure. Some Navajo have embraced pow-wow dancing
(*above*) which has roots in Navajo exposure to urban living.

journey that took them from the First World, which is associated with the color black, to the Second World, which is associated with the color blue, to the Third World, which is associated with the color yellow, and to the present world, called the Glittering World.

In the First World, First Man and First Woman dwelled with different kinds of Insect Beings. There were Spider Ants, Black Ants, Beetles, and Wasp People. Some of the other Insect Beings were Dragon Flies, Bat People, and Spider Man. In this world, evil was known. The People were not in their present human forms. First Man and First Woman met each other in this world, through the fires that they both burned. First Man burned a crystal for fire, and it was the mind's awakening. First Woman burned her turquoise for fire. Crystal was a stronger force than turquoise, and First Woman agreed to live with First Man.

In this First World, the beings disagreed and fought among themselves, and as a result, the entire population emerged into the next world through an opening in the east. In the blue world, these beings found inhabitants living there, including Blue Birds, Blue Hawks, Blue Jays, Blue Herons, and many other feathered beings. There were also locusts and crickets. Before they traveled to this next world, First Man collected four pillars of light and rolled them into small balls, which he carried with him. After a while, they journeyed to the next world, the yellow.

In the yellow world was a great river that crossed the land from north to south—the Female River. The Male River flowed from east to west. This place is called the Crossing of the Waters. In this world there were the six mountains: to the east was Sisnaajiní, which is associated with the Dawn and White Shell; in the south was Tsoodził, called Blue Bead, or Turquoise Mountain; in the west was Dookʼoʼosłííd, called Abalone Shell Mountain; and in the north, Dibé Nitsaa—called Obsidian Mountain. In the center was Dził naʼoodiłii, called Soft Goods or Banded Rock Mountain, and east of center was Chʼóolʼíʼí, also called Precious Stones or Gobernador Knob. There was no sun in this world. Turquoise Boy lived beyond Sisnaajiní to the east, and White Shell Woman lived to the west. Squirrels, Turkeys, Mice, Foxes, Deer, Cat People, and Turkey People also lived here.

Among the beings lived Coyote, well known for his mischievous behavior. Coyote was the one who forced the beings to leave this world because he stole the Water Monster's baby by hiding it in his coat. The rain began to fall, and soon the water rose, causing a great flood. First Man sent word to all the beings, after he heard from the deer and different birds about the flood, to come to Sisnaajiní. He gathered the earth from each of the sacred mountains. The water continued to rise, and First Man planted a cedar tree in hopes that it would reach the sky and they could escape the rising water. Next he planted the pine tree, but like the cedar tree, it did not reach the sky. Next, he planted a male reed and again, it did not grow to reach the sky. Finally, he planted a female reed and it grew to the top of the sky. The beings crowded into the reed and climbed as the water followed them. The Turkey was the last out of the reed and his tail was colored white by the foam of the rushing water. As soon as they emerged into the Fourth World, they noticed that Coyote was hiding something, which turned out to be the Water Monster's baby. Once the baby was returned to the monster, the water began to recede. Water Monster accepted the beings' offering of a white shell basket filled with precious stones, which was placed between his horns.

The beings arrived in the Glittering World, where their interactions with the Holy Deities established the values by which they would live. One of the first things that First Man did was to use the mountain earth he had brought from the lower world to set the boundaries for Diné Bekéyah, Navajo land. The four sacred mountains that established the boundaries of the Navajo homeland are Sisnaajiní or Blanca Peak in the east; Tsoodził or Mount Taylor in the south; Dookʼoʼosłííd or the San Francisco Peaks in the west; and Dibé Nitsaa or Mount Hersperus in the north. The soil brought from the world below also formed two other mountains:

Dził naʼoodiłii or Huerfano Mountain, center; and Chʼóolʼíʼí or Gobernador Knob, east of center.

These last two mountains are within Dinétah, which can be translated as "within the Navajo homeland," and are central to the events that occurred once the progenitors of the Navajo arrived in the Glittering World. Dinétah is considered the original homeland of the Diné, although the creation narratives indicate that the homeland is within the region of the four sacred mountains. Today, Chʼóolʼíʼí lies outside of the official boundaries of the Navajo Nation, even though the site is sacred. Many Navajo, including medicine people, make pilgrimages to the site to conduct prayers.

In her coauthored book of Diné music, Navajo studies educator Marilyn Help shares her favorite songs, including "Shikéyah Nízhónéé Bínáashniih" (Remembering My Beautiful Land). As Help explains, the song embodies the love that the Navajo have for their land and the philosophy that shaped their values and identities as a people. Her own life is shaped by the values embodied in this song, which calls up the stories of the Navajo creation: "The creation story offers a great deal of meaning to me because it teaches me values, values that my grandmother and father have taught me too." Help also shares the special meaning of this song, saying in *We'll Be in Your Mountain, We'll Be in Your Songs: A Navajo Woman Sings*, "The Navajo creation story teaches you discipline; its teachings explain how you should live your life. . . . The creation story teaches self-respect, self-awareness, self-identity, and who you are."

It is in the Glittering World that the Beings evolved into their present human shape, which is the form of the Holy People. Because the human form is that of the Holy Ones, the Navajo are sacred beings. Included in these stories are lessons about what happens when one does not listen to or follow teachings. For example, in one well-known story, First Man returned from a hunting trip one day with deer meat. First Woman prepared a meal with the meat, and after they had finished eating, the couple had a dispute in which First Woman asserted that the women did not need men. First Woman declared that women were perfectly capable of surviving on their own. Outraged, First Man told the other men, who then moved with First Man across the river. The first year, both the men and women fared well. They both planted corn, and although the women did poorly at hunting, they still had enough to eat. Some women would go to the river's edge and taunt the men, who were busy planting their cornfields. After a few seasons apart, the women began to do poorly, as their cornfields were not doing well and they were not very good hunters. Finally, the owl persuaded both sides to reconcile, for if they did not, it would be the end of the people. This story is often cited to point out to the Navajo that both men and women are important to the perpetuation of the People. Men and women must work together for harmony and balance to prevail. Further, as a later chapter will detail, this story is also often cited to discourage women from seeking the highest leadership position in the Navajo Nation, the presidency.

CHANGING WOMAN

In another story of a very important event, First Man was out and about one day and heard an infant crying. Investigating, he came upon a baby girl, whom he took home to his wife, First Woman. They adopted the baby and were so pleased with her that they arranged a Blessingway ceremony to celebrate her birth and to ensure her well-being and prosperity. The Holy People came and brought the songs and prayers that are the foundation of the one-night Blessingway ceremony. The Blessingway embodies all that is significant in Navajo life and is manifested in the concept of Hózhó. Today, the Blessingway continues to be performed to ensure a person's harmony, well-being, and balance.

Under the loving care of First Man and First Woman, the infant who would become Asdzáá Nádleehí, or Changing Woman, thrived. Soon (some people say four days and some say four years), she grew into a young woman. Her passage into womanhood was celebrated with a ceremony, called the Kinaaldá, a puberty rite, which is still performed for girls who have become women. In preparation for the Blessingway, the young woman was adorned in the finest dress and bejeweled with shells and turquoise. Her hair was tied with a length of buckskin, and on her feet were the finest pair of moccasins with buckskin wraps for her legs. Dressed in her finery, she was also known as White Shell Woman. The Holy People came and Haasch'ééłti'í, or Talking God, conducted the ceremony, during which he presented the 12 Hogan songs. The Holy People prayed that Asdzáá Nádleehí would be a fine mother and grandmother. She would head a fine household with plenty of good food to eat and own a sturdy hogan and flocks of horses, sheep, and goats that would sustain her and her children. They prayed that she would take care of the land, always acknowledge its sacredness, and respect the animals and natural elements, like the wind, water, and fire, that were a part of the Navajo world.

Today, a young girl who has reached womanhood might tell her mother or grandmother about having her first menstruation. This sharing sets the Kinaaldá in motion. The young woman's mother or grandmother begins the preparations. They must check on the corn supply because the cake, which will be baked in the ground in a pit prepared for the purpose, can require more than 100 pounds (45 kilograms) of corn. Several generations before, the young woman ground almost all of the corn on a grinding stone by herself. Today, her family might have her grind some of it but take the bulk of the corn to a local corn mill. There must be enough wood to keep a fire going for the duration of the four-day ceremony.

On the first day of the puberty rite, the young woman's father and uncles prepare the pit and start a fire in it. Each day and night the men make sure that the fire does not die out. Her mother will have traveled among her kin and told them of the Kinaaldá, and some of the women will come to witness the hair tying, which officially begins the ceremony. A woman held in high esteem must be asked to serve as the young woman's advisor. Once the young woman's hair is tied, she will begin running, which she must do three times a day until the last morning, after the Blessingway ceremony has been performed. During this time, the young woman must show all the characteristics of Changing Woman. She must show generosity and good cheer. She must be industrious and show that she knows how to care for her hogan, land, livestock, and family.

Finally, on the fourth day, the aunts, grandmothers, and female cousins come together to prepare the corn cake. They spend the better part of a day mixing the corn batter and sewing together corn husks, which will be used to line the bottom of the pit. Another layer is placed upon the batter once it has been poured into the pit. That night, as the cake bakes in the ground and attendants make sure that the fire on top is kept going, the medicine person arrives and the Blessingway begins. In the dawn, after the last song of blessing has been offered, the young woman runs one last time to the east. She has completed a four-day ceremony that required all of her stamina, courage, and goodwill. Her family carefully removes the baked cake from the pit to pass out to the relatives who have come to participate. Generous portions of the cake will go to the medicine person and to those who offered songs throughout the nightlong ceremony. The young woman has received the Holy People's blessings and will take her place as a Navajo woman who has many responsibilities for herself, family, community, and nation.

THE TWIN HEROES

The birth of Changing Woman signaled a new era in Diné; because of her birth, a world of beauty and harmony became possible. Changing Woman, the first mother of the Navajo, is the mother of the most famous twin sons, Nayéé' Neizghání, or Monster Slayer, and Tóbájíshchíní, or Born for Water. Their father is Jóhonaa'éí, the Sun. Like other boys, they loved to play while their mother attended to her chores and daily business. Changing Woman worried about her sons because monsters roamed the land, eating

A grandmother combs and ties her granddaughter's hair before the girl's coming-of-age ceremony, the Kinaaldá. A Navajo girl's coming of age is elaborate and meaningful, as it says she is ready to accept the responsibility that comes with being a woman.

people and drinking all of the water. The people suffered because of the monsters. One day, the boys asked their mother, "Who is our father?" She did not want to tell them, but after the fourth time they asked, she told them that the Sun was their father. The twins wanted to meet their father and prepared for a journey in search of him. Meeting their father for the first time, the twin boys encountered his suspicion, for Jóhonaa'éí did not really know if they were indeed his sons. He also did not want his wife to know that he had been with Changing Woman. To prove that they were his sons, the Sun sent them on several excursions. These excursions were really tests and could have killed Monster Slayer and Born for Water if they had failed. They successfully passed all of the obstacles put before them. In large part, they passed the tests with the help of Grandmother Spider and natural elements like the wind. After they had successfully overcome the obstacles, the Sun presented gifts to them: armors of flint, arrows of lightning, and horses.

Outfitted with warriors' implements, the Hero Twins returned to their mother and came to the aid of the People, who were perishing because of the monsters roaming the land. In one famous case, Monster Slayer came across a monster near present-day Grants, New Mexico, that was killing people and drinking all of the available water. Monster Slayer killed the monster and then cut his head off. To make sure that the monster did not revive, Monster Slayer used his stone knife to make a deep cut in the ground so that the monster's blood would not co-mingle. Today, Navajo remember the story as they pass the blood that has dried into the red rocks that lie just outside of Grants, New Mexico. The story reminds them that warriors are brave and protect the people from harm. After their exploits, the young warriors underwent a purification and healing ceremony, which today is known as the N'da, or the Enemyway.

The stories of the Hero Twins taught young men about how to be a Navajo man and warrior, to be brave and courageous. Just as young women reached a rite of passage with the Kinaaldá, boys also reached manhood when their voices changed and they had a Blessingway ceremony. Today, the most obvious manifestation of what it means to be a warrior is to enlist in the U.S. military. Navajo who join the various branches of the military rely on the stories of the first warriors, the Hero Twins, for courage and protection. The stories of the Hero Twins also explain how soldiers who have seen battle can heal from wartime trauma.

These narratives tell the Navajo of their origins and relationships to the world and to each other. For many families, these stories are the cornerstone of Navajo clans, families, and communities. They have within them prayers and stories about how to live a harmonious life, how to prosper and be healthy, how to raise children properly, how to treat illnesses, how to establish a political community, and how to sustain one's family through livestock raising and agriculture. The stories also tell the Navajo what can happen if they transgress codes of conduct and behavior, how to protect themselves from enemies, and how to purify themselves after going into battle with enemies. Finally, the stories tell them how to treat the world and the animals around them, many of which helped them to survive during the journey through the worlds.

EXPANDING DINÉTAH

According to the stories, the Navajo's ancestors were a simple people who had journeyed through several worlds, emerged into the present world, the Glittering World, and established a way of life based upon the Hózhó. These early Navajo hunted wild animals with simple technology, gathered wild plants for food, and planted fields of corn and squash. Archaeologists and anthropologists agree with the Navajo that Dinétah is the region of early Navajo history and the cradle of Navajo civilization. However, Navajo origins and tenure in the Southwest are still debated among scholars, many of whom declare that those who became Navajo migrated from the north over a period of several hundred years and that much of what is considered "Diné culture" was adopted, adapted, and incorporated from other tribal peoples and non-Native peoples,

Early Governance

Prior to the Euro-American invasion, the Navajo held the balance of power in the Southwest. Non-Indian reports consistently remark upon the autonomy and independence of the People, who were also noted for their wealth as seen in their sheep, goats, horses, and textiles. Beginning with American expansion, the Navajo experienced a loss of their former authority, which began with their incarceration at the Bosque Redondo reservation in 1863. Once the People were allowed to return to their homeland under the Treaty of 1868, Indian agents worked to divest traditional leaders of their power and authority. Today, Navajo Nation leaders and citizens debate what it means to return to a traditional form of governance based upon Navajo philosophy.

Questions that they ask are: "What did Navajo governance look like prior to American colonialism?" and "How can we return to a government based upon traditional teachings?" The traditional Navajo political entity, called a "natural community," was composed of local bands that consisted of 10 to 40 families. In the largest assembly, called a *naachid*, which was a regional gathering, 24 headmen, 12 of whom were peace leaders and 12 of whom were war leaders, met to address internal matters, intertribal affairs, hunting, and food gathering. During years of peace the peace leader presided, and during wartime the war leader presided.

Navajo political organization did not extend beyond local bands, which were led by *naa't'áanii*, or leaders. While leaders were men who were referred to as headmen or chiefs, women could also be naa't'áanii, although that was rare. The political including the Spaniards. Archaeologists and anthropologists have concentrated on questions about the routes the Athapaskan (people from the Artic region) took as they moved southward, the kinds

process was closely tied to ceremonial life, and the naachid served a number of functions, including curing individuals, bringing rain, and restoring the fertility of the soil.

Traditional leaders were selected and served their people based upon their individual abilities and skills. Often medicine people, these leaders served as intermediaries between the People and the Holy People. They were expected to ensure proper behavior, maintain moral injunction such as prohibitions against incest and adultery, and enforce economic laws. They relied upon the elders and the *hataali* (medicine people) for guidance. After a natural community selected a headman, he went through an initiation process that included a Blessingway. The initiation included the anointing of the new leader's lips with corn pollen.

Although Navajo women were not acknowledged as leaders in a Western sense and Americans were confused by Navajo gender norms, Navajo women did play important roles in decision making at every level in their society. Navajo educator Ruth Roessel has noted that Navajo women may not have been appointed as leaders of natural communities, but they were influential when male leaders made decisions on behalf of their people. While few Navajo women appear in non-Indian written accounts of Navajos, two wives of male leaders—Zarcillos Largos and Manuelito—show up in the historical record. An American officer met Zarcillos Largos's wife and noted her sense of authority as she searched for family members lost to slave raiders. Manuelito's wife, who is known in historical and oral accounts as Juanita and by the Navajo as Asdzáá Tł'ógi, was a respected leader among her people. Her husband traveled with her to important council meetings and relied upon her for counsel.

of material culture they brought with them to the Southwest, and what cultural items they borrowed from their Pueblo neighbors.

Another question concerns the extent of cross-tribal relationships so that the Athapaskan population increased. The adoption of livestock also led to the need to expand territory. The preoccupation with migration routes and the formation of the Navajo as a distinctive tribal group often leads to assumptions that the Navajo arrived in the Southwest with a complex language intact, but little else. As historian Peter Iverson remarked in *Diné: A History of the Navajos*, "We have every right to be skeptical about orthodox archaeological accounts in which Navajos arrive essentially intact as a linguistic community, but curiously empty-handed otherwise."

Scholarship is always changing, and in Navajo history one area under scrutiny, which looks to Navajo oral history for answers, is the nature and extent of Navajo relationships with surrounding tribal peoples. For example, questions about their relationships with people who lived at Chaco Canyon in the thirteenth century are being revised, notably through collaborative research efforts by anthropologist Klara Kelley and Navajo scholar Harris Francis. Working with medicine people, Kelley and Francis examined ceremonial prayers and discovered that Navajo prayers map trade routes that move south from the sacred mountains into Mexico, thus raising questions about trade networks that existed between tribal peoples in the Southwest and the length of tenure in the Southwest for the Navajo ancestors.

Scholarship on Navajo relationships to tribal peoples in the pre-Spanish era is changing. For example, Navajo scholar Richard Begay examined Navajo ceremonial knowledge to trace relationships between the Chaco people and Navajo ancestors. He discovered that Navajo ceremonies such as Atásjí (Eagle Way), Hozhónee (Beauty Way), Nílch'jí (Wind Way), Tóee (Water Way), and Yoo'ee (Bead Way) indicate that ancestral Navajo shared knowledge, had kinship, and traded with other pre-Columbian peoples. Importantly, the employment of Navajo oral tradition illuminates

Navajo sacred and historic associations with the land and with pre-Columbian peoples before the appearance of the Spaniards in the sixteenth century. These studies that rely on Navajo oral history also indicate that the process of creation occurred in regions beyond the boundaries of the original Dinétah.

While the Navajo note that some of their ceremonial knowledge came from interaction with the Puebloan people, they also note that their chief ceremony, the Blessingway, is distinctly Navajo, as it was the Holy People who gifted them with the prayers and songs. The Navajo acknowledge relatives in the north; however, they emphasize the ways that their ancestors emerged into the Glittering World and moved about with the intention of living by the Holy People's instructions.

Cycles of Colonialism, 1540–1850

Until fairly recently, scholars have centered their studies of the Southwest within narratives of American expansion, which move from the eastern seaboard into the west. By the time Americans claimed the Southwest as their territory, however, indigenous peoples had been living under foreign rule for more than 200 years. The Navajo are but one group of indigenous peoples who responded to foreign invasions in ways that ranged from caution or resistance to incorporation and adaptation. Non-Indians recorded the transformations that the ancestral Navajo experienced beginning with the Spanish invasion, and even though most reports relied on second- and thirdhand accounts, the Navajo have been depicted as somehow less "indigenous" and somehow "more adaptable" to colonial invasions than other Native peoples.

Nevertheless, the Navajo were transformed by "cycles of conquest"—the changes that indigenous peoples underwent as a result of their exposure to Spanish, Mexican, and then American invasions of the Southwest. Spain and Mexico tried to bring the Navajo under their control. Of Navajo responses, Peter Iverson wrote in *Diné*, "New Spain empowered the Navajos, but its overall relationship with the Diné varied enormously across time and space." By the mid-nineteenth century, when the Americans claimed the Mexican frontier, the Navajo were known as an autonomous people who controlled their own destiny.

This chapter explores Navajo responses to foreign invasions into Diné Bekéyah from the 1540s to the 1850s. Spanish and Mexican documents are sparse in reporting upon the people who became the Navajo; however, what they reported shaped how the Navajo would be seen and responded to for centuries. In the 1820s, American trappers and traders coming into the Southwest characterized the Navajo as freedom-loving people who had resisted Spanish and Mexican colonialism. By the 1850s, however, these favorable reports turned negative as the Americans sought to conquer the Navajo.

In his study *Indian Alliances and the Spanish in the Southwest, 750–1750*, historian William B. Carter remarks upon the prevalence of scholars in portraying "seventeenth-century Navajos and Apaches as pillagers of pueblos, rootless raiders of Spanish settlements and ranches, and hunters marginal to the economic, social, and political developments of colonial New Mexico." Rather, Carter's findings often corroborate Navajo oral history about Navajo geography and the relationships that they had with neighboring tribes, relationships that included alliances, trade, and intermarriage. These findings suggest that the Navajo played important roles in colonial New Mexico and shaped colonial Spain, Mexico, and then the United States.

ARRIVAL OF THE SPANISH

Spanish tenure in its northern frontiers was characterized by three centuries of explorations, settlements, Christianization, and exploitation of the Native peoples and their resources. Hoping to realize fabulous wealth in their northern frontiers, the Spaniards mounted several expeditions beginning in the middle of the sixteenth century, with the first settlement established by Juan de Oñate in 1598. At the time of Oñate's expedition, 81 Pueblo communities lay in three fertile basins: the Estancia Basin in the southern Rio Grande River, the Middle-Rio Grande in present-day Albuquerque-Belen, and the northern Rio Grande River. By 1680, the Pueblo communities had been reduced to 31 with a concentration in the northern Rio Grande basin. Professor Elinore Barrett ventures a number of reasons for the abandonment of Pueblo villages and the decrease in their population, citing Spanish policies and practices that disrupted subsistence activities, as well as forced paid labor, land acquisition, the disruption of trade with other indigenous peoples, and raids by non-Pueblo natives such as the Navajo and Apache.

Although few Spaniards ever saw the Navajo, who stayed close to their well-protected citadels, mesas, and mountainous regions, the presence of the Spanish, and especially the material culture and animals they brought to the New World, dramatically transformed the People. Their presence also shifted the balance of power among tribes and contributed to Navajo migration throughout the four sacred mountains and outlying areas. In 1626, Fray (Friar) Gerónimo de Zárate Salmerón made the first Spanish reference to the "Apache Indians of Navaju." The term has been translated as a Tewa word that means "large area of cultivated fields" and was applied to the ancestral Navajo to distinguish them from their Apache cousins, who did not farm to the same extent as the Navajo.

Three years later, Fray Alonso de Benavides reported that the "Apache Indians of Navaju" occupied lands beyond the frontier of the New Mexican settlements "for another fifty leagues." He estimated that they could assemble 30,000 warriors for war. Benavides's estimate placed Navajo territory west of the Hopi mesas and around the San Francisco Peaks in what is now Arizona. Although conventional scholarship has called Benavides's observations fantasy—both with regards to the population number and the expanse of Navajo territory—other reports of Spanish expeditions into northern Arizona corroborate the presence of indigenous people who may have been ancestral Navajo. Pueblo peoples turned to their neighboring Navajo as early as 1583 when Querechos, probably ancestral Navajo, helped Acoma fight the Spaniards. Pueblo peoples were seeking refuge from Spanish persecution among their Navajo allies as early as 1614 and into the 1620s.

Spanish presence changed the dynamics among the Pueblo villages, as it did for Navajo-Pueblo relationships. For example, bands of Navajo, probably based upon clan and trade relationships, had long-lasting alliances with the Jemez. One early reference by Fray Francisco Pérez Guerta reported that in the spring of 1617, Jemez Indians in concert with some Apache killed an Indian at Cochiti. Several Jemez leaders were brought to Santo Domingo, where one was hanged. The close association of Jemez with their "infidel Apache" brethren was noted when a friar complained that dissatisfied Pueblo Indians fled "to the heathen, believing that they enjoy greater happiness with them, since they live according to their whims, and in complete freedom," David Brugge wrote in "Pueblo Factionalism and External Relations."

The Spanish tradition of slave raiding kept the flames of hostilities alive. Although taking captives was known before Spanish settlement, the practice escalated during the Spanish era and did not end until the late nineteenth century under American rule. This practice was a central point for Navajo attacks on New Mexican settlements, and many expeditions were led into Navajo territory in search of captives. Indeed, the anthropologist Edward Spicer remarked upon the importance of slave raids on the Navajo and Apache as central to ongoing hostilities between these groups, the Pueblo Indians, and New Mexicans. By the 1620s, slave trades were well established, and within decades, most Spanish households and missions possessed Apache, Quiviran, or Ute slaves.

In 1659, Bernardo López de Mendizábal, the governor of New Mexico, ordered raids into Navajo country for women and children, many of whom he sold into Sonora. In 1675 and 1678, the Spaniards ventured into Navajo country in search of victims for their slave trade. Pueblo men joined the Spanish raiders, either because they had been coerced or because they were also being attacked by the Navajo.

PUEBLO REVOLT

A number of factors converged, and after more than 80 years, the Pueblo villages united to drive out the Spaniards. From 1638 to 1660, the Pueblo population decreased by 40 percent, from 40,000 to 24,000. At the same time, the non-Native population almost doubled, from 200 to 400. By 1680, the settler population had reached more than 1,500. Friars reported Pueblo discontent with Spanish policies and warned about Pueblo alliances with the Navajo. On August 10, 1680, after months of planning, the Pueblo Indians rebelled and forced the Spaniards to retreat south to El Paso. As longtime allies of various Pueblos, the Navajo played a pivotal role in the rebellion. For example, Governor Antonio de Otermín claimed that Apaches, including the "Apache Indians of Navaju," throughout the seventeenth century had intended to throw off the Spanish yoke. Otermín also reported a confrontation with a Tano war captain in the first hours of the siege when the captain made several demands, including the release of all Apache men and women captured in war.

In 1692, Diego de Vargas returned to the Rio Grande basin to reestablish Spanish colonies. Historian William Carter characterizes Pueblo responses to the Spanish reappearance as mixed, with some pueblos openly resistant and others showing deference. At several pueblos, Apache, including Navajo, engaged in relationships of trade, alliance, and hostilities, much as they had in early times. One type of relationship with the Pueblo Indians was the creation of clans that resulted from Pueblo women joining and marrying Navajo men. Because Navajo society was and still is matrilineal, a person's identity begins with the mother. Thus, children born of Pueblo women were identified as being of Pueblo descent. For example, clans that link Navajo to Pueblo include the Ma'ii deeshgiizhinii (Jemez), the Naasht'ezhí Dinéé (Zuni), and the Tłʼógi (Zia). The Navajo also have a Mexican clan, which originated when New Mexican women, perhaps captives, married Navajo men and had children, who were of the Nakaii or Mexican clan.

The Spanish campaigns against the Navajo continued into the eighteenth century. After 1705, attempts for peace failed and the Navajo suffered as the Spaniards continued their raids into their country. The Spaniards' presence reconfigured relationships between the Navajo and the Pueblo Indians, some of whom acted as auxiliaries in campaigns against the Navajo. Between 1748 and 1750, two attempts to Christianize the Navajo failed. By the 1750s, Navajo presence was reported south and west of the original Dinétah. Clashes were also inevitable as the Spanish governors issued land grants to their citizens in Navajo territory in the proximity of Mount Taylor. In 1772 Navajos and Apaches formed an alliance and hit settlements along the Rio Grande and Rio Puerco, whereupon New Mexican settlers abandoned the frontier. In 1818, a band of Navajo led by a headman called Joaquin rode into Jemez Pueblo and announced his alliance with the Spaniards. He had convinced his band that peace was the best way to deal with the Spaniards. Of course, the move alienated their kinspeople and thereafter, this group was known as Diné Anaa'í—the Enemy Navajo. Decades later, other leaders of the Diné Anaa'í, such as Francisco Baca and Antonio Sandoval, emerged. Today, their descendants inhabit the community of To'hajiili (formerly known as Canoncito) outside of Albuquerque. To'hajiili is one of the 110 chapters that make up the Navajo Nation.

Between short-lived terms of peace, the Spaniards continued their attempts to pacify the Navajo. One of the best-known campaigns, of which the Navajo still tell stories, is Antonio Narbona's military operation into the Navajo stronghold, the Tséyi' (Canyon de Chelly) in 1805. Narbona's party passed below a cave in which Navajo women, children, and elders were concealed. An elderly woman, who most likely had been a former slave of the Spaniards, and had managed to escape became so incensed at the sight of the soldiers that she began to shout invectives, thereby disclosing their location. The Spanish soldiers fired hundreds of rounds into the cave, killing more than 100 Navajo. That day, in addition to inflicting a massacre, they also took 33 captives.

At the time of Spanish settlement, the ancestral Navajo were concentrated in the Dinétah region, where archaeological remains attest to their presence. Pueblitos, little rock houses, dot the landscape. Remains of forked-stick hogans and sweat lodges are evident on mesa tops. Rock art and paintings depict Holy People and ceremonial art. The evidence of pueblitos has been the source for scholars' conjectures that Pueblo peoples fled Spanish persecution and showed the Navajo how to build the structures. One type of pueblito was built on top of mesas in defensive positions. Scholars argue that the Navajo needed to protect themselves from the Ute and Comanche who were pushing south as a result of foreign invasions from the north and east. It was during that period that horses, sheep, and goats were introduced to the people, animals that became so intertwined with the Navajo that many of the cultural teachings revolve around them. Mounted Navajo warriors ably protected their people from the enemy.

Sheep became prized possessions, so that, even today, the Navajo declare that sheep teach one how to live properly. Life revolved around flocks of sheep and goats, as families moved seasonally to accommodate them. Families were made up of extended families who were related matrilineally. Grandmothers and mothers presided over households, controlled the livestock, and dictated land use. Families followed their sheep to water sources and planted cornfields nearby. In the summer, family

This historic Navajo pictograph panel depicts invading Spanish horsemen. The arrival of Spanish explorers and the horse forever changed Navajo culture.

members moved sheep and goats into the mountainous regions, like the Chuskas and Black Mesa, where there was plentiful grass and water. Others stayed behind to keep watch on the cornfields. The sheep liked the cool air in the mountains, and the children who took care of the sheep also appreciated getting out of the hot weather down below. In the fall the livestock were moved down from the mountains.

Spanish accounts also noted the textiles woven by the Navajo women, which were prized trade items. Used as wearing blankets and clothing, these textiles became so valuable that only wealthy people could afford them, hence the textiles came to be known as "chief's blankets," meaning that those wearing them were people of status. As trade items, these textiles were also an important link between New Mexico and the United States in the Mexican period.

In 1820, Latin American countries were claiming independence from Spain. In Mexico, Agustín de Iturbide concluded the war with Spain and claimed Mexican independence. For the New Mexican settlers, news of Spain's northern frontier becoming Mexican territory had minimal effect, especially as Spain had been unsuccessful in pacifying all of the indigenous peoples, including the Navajo. As Clifford Trafzer wrote of this change in power in *Navajos and Spaniards*, "In fact, news of Mexico's independence did not even send a ripple of excitement to the northern interior" and "the Navajos were little concerned about the change of government in Mexico City, for their war with the soldiers of New Mexico would continue regardless of the flag flying over the capital of the province." In 1822, the Navajo pressed war with the Mexicans.

AMERICAN EXPANSION

In 1845 journalist John O'Sullivan coined a term, "Manifest Destiny," to describe American expansion westward. According to this doctrine, Americans were destined to spread over and claim the continent by the will of God. American citizens and immigrants had long been moving westward before O'Sullivan's declaration, for the prospects of free land drew eager whites toward California and into the Southwest. As early as the 1820s, American travelers made positive reports of the Navajo and often expressed admiration and sympathy for their efforts to resist the Mexican occupiers. In *Commerce of the Prairies*, published in 1844, Josiah Gregg was one who made such remarks, aware that the New Mexicans and their governor had "greatly embittered the disposition of the neighboring savages, especially the Navajos, by repeated acts of cruelty and ill-faith well calculated to provoke hostilities." It had been easy for the Americans to champion the Navajo cause against the Mexicans when they seemed to be on the sidelines, but once they assumed power, their favorable reports quickly turned negative, especially because the Navajo did not welcome the latest invaders. Although the Navajo had good reason to defend their territory, family, and kin, especially because they remained the target of slave raiders, the Americans placed the blame for the cycles of hostilities that characterized the Southwest squarely upon them and the Apache.

Americans faced with subjugating Mexico's former foes now saw the Navajo and the Apache as their enemies, particularly because the Navajo did not see any difference among the waves of conquerors who were determined to bring them under state control. The American takeover of Mexico's northern territories came in 1846 with the arrival of Colonel Stephen Kearny's Army of the West from Fort Leavenworth, Kansas. Beleaguered by continual Navajo attacks and retaliations, Governor Manuel Armijo could simply look on as American forces marched toward Santa Fe.

Upon his arrival into Santa Fe, Kearny announced to the New Mexican populace that he had not come to conquer but, as Clifford Trafzer wrote, "to protect the persons and property of all quiet and peaceable inhabitants . . . against their enemies, the Eutaws, the Navajos, and others." Almost immediately, the Americans recognized that Navajo forces held the balance of power in the Southwest. While the Americans might have announced their claim to the Southwest, Navajo leaders did not immediately acknowledge them. Neither did they visit Santa Fe to meet the American officials. Rather, based on reports of continued clashes between New Mexicans and Navajos, in 1846, Kearny ordered Colonel Alexander Doniphan into Navajo country to ascertain

Navajo acquiescence to American rule. Doniphan's meeting with Navajo leaders, which led to the first treaty signed between Americans and the Navajo, was only one of a series of councils that would end in treaty-signing.

At Ojo Del Oso, or Shush Bitó (Bear Spring), as the Navajo knew the place, Doniphan asserted to the Navajo leaders that the United States claimed New Mexico by right of conquest and that it would protect all of its new citizens, including the Navajo. He noted the ongoing war between New Mexicans and Navajos and emphasized to the leaders that their attacks on New Mexicans must cease or they would face war with the United States. On behalf of the Navajo contingent, the respected headman Zarcillos Largos answered with the eloquent and powerful oratory for which Navajo leaders were known. His people had just cause for their war against the New Mexicans, for they had lost many of their women and children to the slave trade. According to Frank McNitt's *Navajo Wars: Military Campaigns, Slave Raids, and Reprisals*, Largos said, "You have lately commenced a war against the same people. You are powerful. You have great guns and many brave soldiers. You have therefore conquered them, the very thing we have been attempting to do for so many years." He chastised the Americans, "You now turn upon us for attempting to do what you have done yourselves. We cannot see why you have cause of quarrel with us for fighting the New Mexicans on the west, while you do the same thing on the east." He ended his declarations with an entreaty: The Americans should allow the Navajo to settle their disputes with the New Mexicans.

Largos's speech attests to the Navajo's perceptions of their own place in the Southwest. In the nineteenth century, Navajo leaders saw themselves as the Americans' equals, if not their superior. Largos also acknowledged the Americans' superior firepower and raised questions about the nature of American interest in the Southwest, for it was clear to the Navajo that, like the Mexicans, the Americans were determined to claim the Southwest at whatever cost to the Navajo. Nevertheless, on November 22, 1846, the first of nine treaties was agreed upon between the Americans and Navajo leaders. The treaty called for a lasting peace between the two parties, trade, and the restoration of property and citizens to each side. However, the failure of the Americans to enforce the provision to have the Navajo women and children returned to them would remain a point of contention far into the latter part of the nineteenth century.

One signatory to the treaty was Manuelito, the son-in-law of the revered leader Narbona. At 28 years of age, Manuelito was young for a *naa'táani*, a leader. According to oral tradition, at the news of his birth, Manuelito's father had come, taken the newborn into the sunlight, and presented him to the Holy People. He prophesized that his son would be a great warrior whose skills would protect his people and that his words would be taken to heart. Manuelito was accustomed to being around leaders in his early life. His father, Cayetano was a known resistor to foreign rule. His brother Cayetanito, one of the leaders to go to Washington, D.C., in 1874, was prominent in the Mount Taylor area. Two other brothers, K'ayelli (One with Quiver) and El Ciego (the Blind One), also followed Manuelito's lead.

The treaty of Ojo Del Oso did not stand long as conflict between the Navajo and New Mexicans was almost immediate. Between 1847 and 1849, warfare continued unabated, and Kearny's proclamation that civilians could continue their war upon the Navajo if their women, children, and livestock had been seized heightened the hostilities. Reports of Navajo depredations on New Mexican settlements poured into Santa Fe. After several excursions into Navajo country failed to end hostilities, especially as conflict renewed eight months after American officials had signed a second treaty with Navajos, Col. John Washington proceeded with plans to control the Navajo.

Taking 178 soldiers, 123 New Mexico volunteers (slave raiders), and 60 Pueblo scouts, Washington left Santa Fe for Navajo

The Many Names of Manuelito

Best known to non-Indians as Manuelito, this Navajo warrior was known to his people by several names. These include `Ashkii Diyinii (Holy Boy), Naabaahii Jóta' (Warrior Grabbed Enemy), Naabáána baadaaní (son-in-law of the late Texan), and Hastin Ch'il Hajin (Man from Black Weeds).

Manuelito's names mark events and places in his life. "Holy Boy" indicates that he was blessed and recognized as a warrior by the Holy People. "Naabáána badaaní" means that he was the son-in-law of the peace leader Narbona, a revered leader among the Navajo. The name "Hastin Ch'il Hajin" indicated the place he lived, probably during the American period, a place known as Black Weeds. The name "Manuelito" was assigned by Mexicans, and the Americans continued to call him by that name.

country. On August 30, 1849, the military expedition camped near Tunicha Creek, north of present-day Naschitti, New Mexico, and near Copper Pass (now known as Narbona Pass). One of the men with Washington penned his observations of being in Navajo country. The people were far from being the "savages" that white men called them, and Navajo fields of corn and wheat could be seen. Several Navajo leaders approached Washington's camp. Washington immediately accused them of stealing livestock and killing New Mexican citizens. The leaders responded in much the same manner as they had in earlier communications with the foreigners and as they would in the future. The headmen did not have control of all of their people and yes, there were lawless men among them, but they wanted peace and were willing to make some retribution in livestock. Washington requested that the two parties negotiate a treaty the following day and said he would travel to Tséyi' (Canyon de Chelly) to sign the treaty formally.

The Navajo leaders returned the following day. Among them was the aging Narbona, who was widely known for his efforts to keep peace. The Navajo congregation also turned over livestock as a sign of good faith. The treaty negotiations commenced with Narbona representing the Navajo. At the end of the meeting, the Navajo headman explained that he would not be at the formal treaty signing but would send two other leaders, Armijo and Pedro José, to which Washington agreed. Then the Navajo leader Antonio Sandoval began to speak. Sandoval and his people lived the closest to the New Mexican settlements and so he sought compromises with the Americans to ensure the safety of his band. He and his people had a history of alliances with the New Mexicans and had stolen his own Navajo people for the slave trade. Now, he accompanied the Americans and acted as the translator for the proceedings between the two parties. For good reason his fellow Navajo did not trust him. Sandoval's harsh speech stirred the Navajo warriors, and the disturbance was compounded when a New Mexican with the military claimed that his stolen horse was among the Navajo.

Washington ordered the Navajo to return the horse immediately. Chaos threatened as the Navajo leaders tried to calm their men. The American commander ordered his riflemen to begin firing upon the Navajo. As the soldiers did, many Navajo fought back while others fled. When the pandemonium subsided, Narbona lay dead from multiple wounds. Narbona's murder was especially outrageous to his people because he had counseled peace with the Americans. Six other Navajo also died, while the military expedition lost only a few horses. Of Narbona's murder, Washington reported to his superiors that the head chief of the nation had been a scourge to New Mexico's inhabitants for the last 30 years. As historian Frank McNitt noted, however, Washington's assertion about Narbona was simply untrue.

FORT DEFIANCE

In hopes of seeing peace, the Navajo leaders signed a third treaty with Americans on September 9, 1849. Its provisions called for the Navajo to surrender livestock taken from the settlements, promised free passage across Navajo country, and permitted the U.S. government to establish military and trading posts on Navajoland. The leaders' agreement to allow the establishment of forts set the stage for unremitting warfare and unimaginable suffering when Colonel Edwin Sumner established Fort Defiance in the heart of Navajo territory in 1851. Over the span of several years, Navajo leaders objected, especially to American claims to prime grazing

Navajo stand at Fort Defiance, Arizona, circa 1873. Disputes over grazing lands near Fort Defiance led to war between the Navajo and the U.S. Army.

lands surrounding the fort. In particular, Manuelito claimed the lands for his own use, and the dispute with the U.S. Army led to war in 1858. Manuelito's challenge to the Americans was pivotal, as McNitt wrote in *Navajo Wars*, the "final and fateful turning point in [white] relations with the Navajo nation," in which an unfolding set of conflicts ended only with Manuelito's bitter defeat and his captivity at the Bosque Redondo.

In 1857, Major William Thomas Harbaugh Brooks assumed command at Fort Defiance. Manuelito did not immediately come to the fort to visit the new commander, making Brooks wonder about the state of their relations with the Navajo. When the leader did come, the major described Manuelito's visit, writing to his superiors that the headman had informed him that the Navajo would allow the military to graze their livestock at Ewell's camp. Upon visiting the site, however, Brooks discovered that Manuelito meant to keep at least half of the lands for his own use, much to his displeasure. Brooks also noted that Manuelito gave notice that he was resigning as chief and had sent a messenger with the baton and medal, signatories of office, to Brooks, which he refused. Several days later, on a day set aside to distribute farming implements to the Navajo, 300 to 400 Navajo appeared, including the headmen Zarcillos Largos and Hijo de Juanico. Brooks, noting that Largos did not stop to talk with him, requested reinforcements, for it seemed to him that conflict was inevitable.

Manuelito and his men continued to challenge the Americans for the grazing fields surrounding the fort. On April 5, 1858, a Captain Hatch encountered Manuelito and Largos with a large force of warriors. Manuelito delivered 117 sheep to the captain and said that the remainder of the sheep had been killed, sold, or distributed among the Navajo. The reports from this period repeatedly note that the Navajo attempted to return sheep and other livestock that other Navajo had taken. While some Navajo were indeed raiding the New Mexican settlements, many others had no hand in depredations. The captain turned back, fearing an attack with such a large show of force by the Navajo. On May 29, Brooks's men tried to drive out the Navajo flocks, many of which belonged to Manuelito. Witnessing their attempts, Manuelito approached the fort with his men and addressed Brooks. He told the major that the water, grass, and grounds around the military post belonged to him and that "he was born and raised there, and that he would not give it up." Brooks replied that he would retain the military's use of the lands even if it meant using force. That night, his soldiers went to the field and slaughtered Navajo livestock.

Following the slaughter of Manuelito's livestock, the U.S. Army kept a wary eye on Manuelito and other Navajo leaders. Brooks noted that, the day after the livestock were killed, Largos came to the fort and said that he was for peace and that Manuelito had been foolish for insisting on ownership of the grazing lands. Brooks handed Manuelito's baton to Largos, indicating that it had been found in the field where the cattle were killed. Largos told Brooks about Navajo leaders sending a request to Santa Fe for reimbursement for Manuelito's livestock.

A TURNING POINT

The murder of Brooks's black slave Jim, interpreted by many historians as retribution for the loss of Manuelito's cattle, served as a pivotal point for an all-out war on the Navajo. One day a Navajo man, reportedly from Cayetano's band, came to the fort and tried to sell a blanket. After a few hours inside the encampment, he suddenly took aim and shot Brooks's slave. In a report to his superiors, Brooks wrote that on July 12 a Navajo man had come into the fort and fired an arrow at Jim. The wounded Jim, according to Brooks's report, "never uttered a word or exclamation, but attempted to pull the arrow out, in doing which he broke it off near the head." The doctor was unable to extract the head of the arrow from Jim's body. He died four days later.

Enraged by the seeming impunity of the Navajo, Brooks insisted that the perpetrator be brought to him for American justice. A southerner, Brooks believed that Jim was property and that his property had been destroyed. He also believed that the "colored" races were inferior and that the strong arm of the white man would teach them their proper place.

With Brooks's continued demands for the man who had killed his slave, the Navajo eventually brought in the body of the man they said had killed Jim. The army surgeon's examination showed that it was not the man they sought. Further enraged at Navajo resistance, Brooks notified his superiors that he had given the Navajo more than adequate time to hand over the culprit. He wrote, "Our duty remains to chastise them into obedience to our laws—After tomorrow morning war is proclaimed against them."

Brooks's insistence that the man who killed his slave be turned over to him, coupled with reports of Navajo raids on New Mexican communities, led to a series of battles over the course of four months. The battles were costly to the Navajo: At least 200 of their warriors were killed while the U.S. troops saw far fewer fatalities. Once again, perhaps to temporarily halt conflicts with the Americans, the Navajo leaders signed yet another treaty at Fort Defiance. This treaty, negotiated and signed by Colonels B. L. E. Bonneville and James L. Collins for the United States and 15 Navajo leaders, including Manuelito, established an eastern boundary for Navajo land, payment of indemnification by the tribe for depredations committed by the Navajo, the release of all captives by both parties, and waiver of the demand for the surrender of the murderer who touched off the war. The United States also demanded the right to send expeditions through Navajo country and to establish military posts. The U.S. Senate, however, did not ratify this treaty.

On April 30, 1860, Manuelito and Barboncito led an attack on Fort Defiance. In the early morning, about 1,000 warriors stormed the fort. They were unsuccessful, largely because the three companies inside the fort had superior firepower. The attack caused New Mexicans and the army alike to agree that it was necessary to make war on the Navajo. As one New Mexican citizen declared, as cited in *The Army and the Navajo*, it was not possible to change the Navajo: "You might as well make a hyena adopt the habits of a poodle dog."

The attack on Fort Defiance renewed New Mexicans' daring, and they ventured into Navajo country to capture women and children. On one foray the raiders, who included Zuni auxiliaries, came across Zarcillos Largos, whom they promptly murdered. Largos's death was a great loss for the Navajo, for he had been greatly respected for his avocations for peace. Indeed, during a *naachid*—the largest council in which the People gathered to decide matters concerning all—24 leaders pondered the case for war or peace with the Americans. Largos had argued eloquently for peace. He had entreated the people to listen to his message, for he had had a dream about the ruins that war would bring them. Manuelito, however, dressed for war, had carried the day with his oratory. The people found his message compelling, and with the consensus to press against the American aggressors, they rushed back to their residences knowing that war was inevitable.

Another disturbance occurred on September 22, 1861, at Fort Fauntleroy, which was established near present-day Fort Wingate. As part of a campaign to gain Navajo trust, the commander distributed rations. The distribution days were festive, and Navajo and whites alike bet on horse races and card games. On one of these occasions, more than 300 Navajo gathered at Fauntleroy in anticipation of a peace council. As part of the activities, a horse race was proposed. For several days, the soldiers bet on their favorite, the horse of the post's assistant surgeon, with great results. On September 22, Manuelito brought his horse to race. During the race, Manuelito's horse left the track, and it was discovered that its bridle had been cut. The Navajo demanded another race, but the soldiers refused. When the Navajo protested, the soldiers opened fire on the crowd.

REMOVAL AND RELOCATION

With the beginning of the Civil War began in 1861, many soldiers left for the South. Cycles of violence continued to characterize the Southwest. In the 1830s, President Andrew Jackson had set forth federal policy for dealing with Native peoples who challenged the American thirst for their lands and resources. The Indian Removal Act paved the way for the removal and relocation of indigenous peoples who stood in the way of settlers. In the South, the first victims of the act—the Cherokee, Chickasaw, Choctaw, Creek, and Seminole—were forcibly removed from their homelands to Indian Territory, in present-day Oklahoma. Following this policy, General Edward R. S. Canby advocated for Navajo removal from their homeland but was consumed with the Civil War and so left its implementation to James Carleton, who took command upon Canby's departure. Paramount to General Carleton's interest in removing the Navajo were reports of gold.

Carleton's plans included removal of the Mescalero Apache, who were also seen as threats to continued settlement. Considering several areas to establish a reservation, he finally settled on a place adjacent to Fort Sumner in east-central New Mexico. Ignoring reports that the area was largely uninhabitable, the water alkaline, wood scarce, and the summers and winters harsh, Carleton outlined his plan. At the Bosque Redondo, Navajo and Mescalero would be grouped into villages and learn the arts of civilization. They would become farmers and be instructed in Christian virtues, and their children would be educated in American ways.

As cited in *Navajo Roundup: Selected Correspondence of Kit Carson's Expedition Against the Navajos, 1863–1865*, Carleton declared to his superiors that force was necessary to bring the Navajo under control, for they could "no more be trusted than you can trust the wolves that run through their mountains." If the army placed them on a reserve far "from the haunts and hills and hiding places of their country, and there be kind to them," they would "acquire new habits, new ideas, new modes of life." Carleton noted that it was impossible to retrain the older Indians, but possibilities for their "civilization" lay with the children: "The young ones will take their places without these longings: and thus, little by little, they will become a happy and contented people." By September 1863, Carleton laid down his orders: All captives who surrendered voluntarily would go to the Bosque Redondo. All male Navajo who resisted would be shot. Those who surrendered would be given food, clothing, and shelter and then await orders to journey to the Bosque Redondo.

To force the Navajo's surrender and remove them to the reservation, Carleton enlisted the renowned Indian fighter Kit Carson to convey his message. Carson was known by many Native peoples, for he had not only served as a guide for settlers coming west, but also as an Indian agent in the service of the federal government. Before Carson's campaign, the army had been hapless to force Navajo surrender. Not only did the Navajo know their country so well that they could call upon the Holy People and the natural world for protection, but Tséyi' with its high canyon walls proved to be an impenetrable fortress. Also inside the canyon was Spider Rock, a towering needle-like rock formation, which served as a haven. Once the Navajo climbed up its steep sides on yucca ladders and pulled up the ladders, it was impossible to reach them.

In the summer of 1863, Carson began his campaign against the Navajo. Moving with 221 men from Los Lunas to Fort Wingate, he added 326 men to his command. In his first attempts to force the Navajo to surrender, Carson was unsuccessful. By the fall, Carson had failed to engage the Navajo in open conflicts; rather, the warriors who followed the militia, taking livestock and attacking army herds, continually embarrassed Carson's men. Finally, using scorch and burn tactics, Carson fed his soldiers and livestock on Navajo wheat and corn and then destroyed the rest of the harvest. He and his men destroyed every hogan they came across. Livestock was slaughtered and their carcasses left to rot.

Spider Rock is an 800-foot (244-meter) spire that stands in the heart of Canyon de Chelly. According to Navajo legend, it was the home of Spider Woman. Spider Rock was a safe haven for the Navajo when they were under attack by U.S. troops.

The peach trees lining the canyon floors were slashed. His war was indiscriminate—targeting women and children and allowing volunteers to take captives as payment. Carson's men also humiliated and murdered Navajo who surrendered. As a result of the abuse they suffered and because stories circulated of Navajos being murdered, many refused to surrender. As Clifford Trafzer noted in *Kit Carson's Campaign*, the Navajo were convinced that Carson's campaign was a war of extermination: "Thus the Indians felt that they had no choice but to remain fast in their mountains and to avoid the onslaught of the troops, who they feared would murder them if they surrendered."

After months of failure, and with the winter approaching, Carleton ordered Carson to continue the war with an invasion of the Navajo stronghold, Tsé yi'. The Navajo recall this time in their history as "the fearing time," when their people were on the run from the soldiers, for it was a nightmarish time. It seemed to the Navajo that all of their enemies, including the Ute, the Zuni, and other Pueblo peoples had been unleashed on them. Eli Gorman said that Biʼéé Łichííʼí (Carson), which translates as Red Shirt, kept the Navajo on the run. Carson did not discriminate between peaceful and hostile Navajo: Peaceful Navajo were picked up and many were killed. Children were sold into slavery. Many who surrendered and entered the fort were ashamed of the state they were in. Some arrived with hardly a stitch of clothing, and the soldiers gave them a piece of cloth to cover their nakedness. Carson's forays into the stronghold proved too much for the Navajo, who had been severely weakened by his scorch and burn tactics.

By late 1863, thousands of Navajo, destitute and starving, surrendered at the American forts. Delgadito, one of the first headmen to capitulate, and 187 of his people came in late November 1863. After a time, Delgadito and three other Navajo took Carleton's message to Diné Bekéyah: The People must surrender and move to the Bosque Redondo reservation, where they would be able to live in peace. Delgadito said that he had spoken personally to the American general and that the Navajo would be shown no mercy if they continued to resist. At the end of January 1864, Delgadito arrived at Fort Wingate with 680 Navajo.

In March 1864, General Carleton reported to his commander that more than 3,000 Navajo had surrendered at Fort Canby and would join the other prisoners at the Bosque Redondo, bringing the total number of Navajo captives to 6,000. The campaign was winding down; however, the attacks against the Navajo did not cease as slave raiders found it profitable to continue their raids. Although the military was finding it impossible to care for its prisoners, Carleton was still eager to get Manuelito and Barboncito to surrender. The *Santa Fe Gazette* published an officer's report about the need to capture or kill Manuelito. Manuelito was so influential that his capture or death would mean the final defeat. In early August 1864, soldiers surprised Barboncito and his people, who were in Canyon de Chelly. The leader surrendered with the remainder of his kin, which numbered only five men, a woman, and a child. Although he made the journey to the prison camp, he left within the year with a group of his people and lived among Apache allies in their mountains. However, he surrendered once again and arrived at Fort Sumner in November 1866.

TRACKING DOWN MANUELITO

In the spring of 1864, military officers received word that Manuelito would turn himself in. Manuelito appeared at Fort Canby but refused to go to the Bosque Redondo. An officer told him that he had but one choice and that was to go to Hwéeldi, which was what the Navajo called Bosque Redondo. Learning about conditions at the reservation, Manuelito requested a visit from Herrera, one of the chiefs at the internment camp. In a report dated March 21, 1865, Carleton related the results of Herrera's meeting with Manuelito. Herrera explained that Manuelito was in poor condition, that he had about 50 people with him, and that he had few horses and sheep. As cited in J. Lee Correll's *Through White Men's Eyes*, Manuelito said, "Here is all I have in the world. See what a trifling amount. You see how poor they are. My children are eating roots." Herrera reported that Manuelito refused to surrender and reminded Herrera that their people should never cross the Rio Grande River or go beyond the sacred mountains. He would remain in his homeland and suffer the consequences. At their kinsman's declarations, the women in his camp began to cry in distress. Throughout 1865 and into 1866, Manuelito and his band eluded the Americans and New Mexican and Ute slave raiders. In 1866, after thousands of his fellow Navajo had surrendered to the Americans and had been forced to endure the "Long Walk," Manuelito finally admitted defeat. Wounded and ill, the great warrior led his remaining kin to Fort Wingate, where they were to await a military escort to Hwéeldi. With him were around 50 of his band, probably including his wife, Juanita, and their children.

Kit Carson's war on the Navajo led to the next phase, as thousands of Navajo had surrendered at Forts Defiance and Wingate, where they awaited orders to be removed to the Bosque Redondo reservation. By the winter of 1863, Carson's campaign against the Navajo was over. The next chapter details the Long Walk and captivity at the Bosque Redondo reservation, from 1863 to 1868. Although the Navajo were overpowered by the military might of the U. S. government, and met a fate similar to other Native peoples, their story is also unique in that they insisted upon their rights to live as they wished and returned to their homeland against great odds. Stories of their ancestors' experiences under extreme oppression inspire the Navajo to claim a unique history. They hope that knowing this history will help them reclaim a distinctively Navajo heritage and bolster their effort to realize true sovereignty.

The Long Walk and Hwéeldi

The Long Walk and the years at Hwéeldi are watersheds in Navajo history, for they mark the separation between a time when the Navajo were an autonomous people who held the sway of power in the Southwest for at least 200 years and a time when they were militarily defeated and rendered dependent on the U.S. government. This chapter explores the Navajo experience under U.S. policies of forced removal and relocation to a reservation where the captives were subjected to the American assimilation program. For the Navajo, this time in their history was so traumatic and horrific that many refused to speak of their experiences for decades.

Their stories, however, are etched in the Navajo collective memory, and even after nearly 150 years, they have the capacity to bring strong emotions to the surface. Upon sharing these stories of their ancestors, Navajo mourn and express shock at the United States'

capacity for violence toward its indigenous peoples. For decades, until the 1950s, the stories remained private, and the Navajo refused to speak of what happened to their grandmothers and grandfathers. As the Navajo elder Mary Pioche said, "When men and women talk about Hwéeldi, they say it is something you cannot really talk about, or they say that they would rather not talk about it. Every time their thoughts go back to Hwéeldi, they remember their relatives, families, and friends who were killed by the enemy."

In December 1862, the fledging Fort Sumner consisted of tents and housed six officers and 133 enlisted men. The site's flaws, combined with other factors—such as its distance from a supply center like Fort Union; the constant shortage of food for the Navajo and Apache captives; the continued hostilities among Navajo, Apache, and New Mexicans; the dreary weather—would all be part of the recipe for the failure of "Fair Carletonia." In the end, General James Carleton was forced to admit failure. For four years, 400 Mescalero Apache and 11,000 Navajo eked out a living at the Bosque Redondo reservation. Ultimately, both the Mescalero and the Navajo returned to their own country.

Two kinds of accounts provide valuable information about the Navajo experience during the Long Walk and the years at Hwéeldi. On the one hand, military reports detail day-to-day operations of carrying out federal Indian policy and appear to be objective and aloof. On the other hand, Navajo oral tradition, which often contradicts the written military reports, makes vivid the horror and terror the captives felt. The stories cause modern Navajo to thank their ancestors for surviving U.S. expansion into the west and bolster the determination to realize Navajo sovereignty.

CARAVANS OF PRISONERS

One category of narrative details the end of war in late 1863 as thousands of Navajo surrendered at the forts established in their territory. Once at the forts, they awaited orders to begin the long march to the Bosque Redondo. Although the experience is called "the Long Walk," in fact, historian Neal Ackerly has counted at least 53 forced marches that began at either Fort Defiance or Fort Wingate. Once a caravan of captives was organized, the forced march began, from either fort. This ordeal was hell on earth. As caravans of prisoners reached Albuquerque, several different routes were taken. The earlier groups traveled past Santa Fe and Galisteo and went on to Fort Union in northern New Mexico. The Fort Union route, beginning at Fort Canby, was the longest of the trails at 425 miles (684 kilometers). By the shortest route, and the one that was infrequently used, the Navajo prisoners faced a march of 375 miles (604 km). The mountain route, which extended east

Bosque Redondo was the end destination of the Long Walk, the removal of the Navajo from their homeland. There, the U.S. government intended to turn Navajo into farmers, educate them in Western ways, and convert them to Christianity. Above, a group of Navajo who were imprisoned at the Bosque Redondo reservation.

from Albuquerque through Tijeras Canyon and turned north along the eastern slopes of the Sandias and into Galisteo, became the most frequently used route after Kit Carson's sweep of the Navajo fortress. At Galisteo, the prisoners then proceeded to Fort Union. From there, they headed to the Bosque Redondo.

The first group of captives started for the Bosque Redondo when Carson's summer campaign of 1863 was in its opening phase. Around August 6, Capt. Albert H. Pfeiffer captured eight Navajo, including five women and children. The captives were taken to Fort Canby and then to Fort Wingate, where 43 Navajo from the Diné Anaa'í Sandoval's band joined the captives. Although the Diné Anaa'í had allied with the New Mexicans and then the Americans, they were among the first to be relocated to the reservation on the Pecos River. The commander in charge of getting this group to the Bosque Redondo had his orders: If any captives tried to escape, they were to be shot. None did. On September 2, the captives passed through Santa Fe. Santa Fe's newspaper, the *Weekly Gazette*, noted the captives: "We presume they will be transferred to some military post to the East of this, and there retained separated from . . . the balance of the tribe to the end of the war." On September 7, the prisoners arrived at Fort Union, where it was reported that a child had died. During these marches, hundreds of children died; their numbers add to those who perished with Carleton's war. The death of a woman was also reported. Twenty-four days after their departure from Fort Wingate, they arrived at Hwéeldi; they were allowed two days of rest during the march.

Three months later, on December 10, the headman Delgadito and about 200 captives arrived at the reservation. Fifteen of his band were missing and had probably been stolen by slave raiders. Leaders like Delgadito surrendered alongside their people and tried to alleviate their suffering. They were sources of hope and inspiration. Delgadito and his band left Wingate under the command of Captain Rafael Chacon; upon reaching the outskirts of Santa Fe, Lieutenant V.B. Wardwell assumed responsibility.

Wardwell submitted a report, which is one of a few that provide a detailed account of the captives' daily movements. As they arrived near Santa Fe, the temperature dropped below freezing and a storm shrouded the route ahead. Each day the captives traveled eight to ten miles (12.8 to 16 km). The first night outside of Santa Fe, they made camp in the hills east of the town. Succeeding stops were made at Kozlowski's Ranch, San José, Tecolote, Las Vegas, William Kroenig's Ranch on Sapello Creek, and then about two and a half miles (4 km) southwest of Watrous. At Fort Union Captain William P. Calloway assumed responsibility for the captives and forced them onto the last leg of the journey. At the fort, fellow Navajo welcomed Delgadito and his band with a display of emotion.

Soon after, Carleton instructed Delgadito and three other men to return to Navajo country with his message that all Navajo must surrender or be treated without mercy. The headman told his fellow Navajo that he had been to the Bosque Redondo, and compared to the countless number of Navajo dying in their own country, the newly created reservation was a sanctuary. At the end of January, Delgadito arrived at Fort Wingate with 680 Navajo, and a few days later, around 500 more joined them. Delgadito reported that, along the trail to the fort, a party attacked his people and captured women, children, and livestock. Several warriors were also killed.

STORIES OF SURVIVAL

Hundreds of Navajo stories like Chahadineli Benally's have survived and provide valuable information from Navajo perspectives. Benally was 85 years old when he told his grandmother's story. Before 1863, Benally's relatives lived near Black Mesa in northern Arizona. One day, the young woman who would become his grandmother was looking for food with her little brother when a group of Mexicans on horseback suddenly appeared. In vain, the young pair tried to hide, but it was too late. The Mexicans had spied them and then captured them. The raiders traveled past Ganado and Klagetoh with their captives. Once they passed beyond the Navajo homeland, the land appeared strange to the frightened pair. Each night as the group made camp, the woman did her best to comfort her frightened brother.

Eventually, the travelers reached their destination, and the woman became a servant to a Mexican family. The woman of the household befriended her and noticed the young woman's pregnancy. Her new friend was incensed that the young Navajo woman had been stolen from her family and was deeply disturbed when she learned that her husband planned to sell her to another household. Unbeknownst to her husband, the Mexican woman helped her new friend escape. Fleeing across the strange land, the young woman gave birth. Near starvation and extremely weak, she was forced to abandon her newborn infant, whom she never forgot. The boy was never heard from again.

Howard Gorman of Ganado, Arizona, also shared stories from his family, as cited in *Navajo Stories*. As Kit Carson's army moved through Navajoland, it destroyed sheep, horses, and waterholes. Gorman's family walked all night to reach the safety of Tséyi'. Upon reaching the canyon walls, they stopped and made a fire. The steps leading into the canyon were slippery with ice, so the exhausted group settled down for the night. Their stop enabled the soldiers, who were being guided by a Navajo man, to catch up with them. The Navajo fought back, and that day, many died. One man named Preparing a Warrior escaped by jumping into the canyon. He landed on some bushes and ran to safety. In the melee, a child strapped in a cradle was left behind. The cradle saved the baby girl from physical harm. One man was wounded and taken captive. He was warned that, if he and the others did not immediately surrender, Carson's men would kill them. With that message, 16 Navajo surrendered. They knew that resistance was fruitless because Ute warriors had also joined the New Mexican volunteers and were looking to kill them.

Keyah David shared a story of the forced marches and how a couple was having trouble keeping up with the rest of the group because their infant was growing weaker and weaker. The wife could not keep up, while her husband urged her to walk faster. He feared the dangers of being left behind. Finally, out of desperation, he entreated his wife to abandon the child, for it seemed that he would not live much longer. When she refused, he said angrily, as quoted in *The Changing Ways of the Southwestern Indians: A Historic Perspective*, "All right, stay there if you like, but I'm going on. The baby is going to die anyway." As the man hurried to catch up to the group, he had an idea. After breaking off stalks of cactus oozing juice, he returned to his wife and their baby and fed the liquid to the infant. The infant stirred, the father broke off more cactus stalks, and with his family, hurried to catch up with the slow-moving caravan.

In his testimony for the Land Claims Commission in 1951, John Daw reported stories he learned from his parents. Along the march, when people became exhausted and pleaded with the soldiers to slow down, the soldiers became harsh and rebuffed them. If a prisoner persisted, he was shot to death. Daw also noted the violence done to the women: "These soldiers did not have any regard for the women folks. They took unto themselves for wives somebody else's wife, and many times the Navajo man whose wife was being taken tried to ward off the soldiers, but immediately he was shot and killed and they took his wife." John Bowman, who also testified before the commission, reported, "The children would get exhausted from the day's walk and want to ride on these wagons . . . and if the children were a little bit too large or a little older and able to walk, the soldiers would just cast them aside and make them walk until the time came when they would dispose of them." These stories are filled with such pain, humiliation, and degradation that those who hear them cannot help but reflect upon the lengths that the Navajo went to in order to survive.

ODD NEW FOODS

It was at the forts, where they awaited transportation to the Bosque Redondo, that the People were first introduced to strange foods—white flour, pork, beans, sugar, and coffee—which then became staples at the new reservation. Before the introduction of these foods, the Navajo prepared all sorts of corn dishes, including puddings, cakes, breads, steamed corn on the cob, and stews. Berries made excellent puddings, while dried squash rinds cut into rings and peaches were stored for later use. Local herbs, wild onions, and celery were used in all sorts of dishes. In the fall, piñon nuts were collected, roasted, and stored. Because they preferred to keep their wealth on the hoof, they rarely butchered a goat or sheep for meat. When they did, no part of the animal was wasted. To add variety to their diets, they hunted deer and antelope and jerked venison for winter use.

Unaccustomed to these new rations, the Navajo learned how to prepare them through trial and error and by asking their captors. Sometimes the strange food made them sick. They ate the white flour by mixing it with water to make a mush. Often the flour was stale and filled with bugs and even plaster. So they fried the dough to make it edible. (Ironically today, "fried bread," a favorite with Navajo and tourists alike, is considered a "traditional" Navajo food.) They boiled the coffee beans and waited for them to soften so they could eat them as a soup. They threw away the dark water and ate the coffee beans. The beef and pork was often rancid and inedible. The foods caused many to die from diarrhea and dysentery.

TOO MANY CAPTIVES

By early 1864, the number of Navajo surrendering at the forts reached such proportions that the army found itself ill-prepared. As cited in *Through White Men's Eyes*, on February 27, Carleton reported to Gen. Lorenzo Thomas in Washington, "What with the Navajoes I have captured and those who have surrendered we have now over 3,000, and will, without doubt, soon have the whole tribe. . . . You have doubtless seen the last of the Navajo war, a war that has been continued with but few intermissions for 180 years." He declared that "this formidable band of robbers and murderers have at last been made to succumb." Because of the large numbers, Carleton ordered the caravans to travel the mountain route. The captives found a bit of relief because the arroyos, narrow valleys, and canyons between the mountains and mesas provided some shelter from the winter elements. Water and wood were found in adequate supply. Also, for the army's purposes, this route made it possible to access emergency supplies and surveillance was easier for the garrisons.

Several other large contingents of prisoners also marched along this route. In February 1864 a train of nearly 1,500 men, women, and children traveled this route. Following on the heels of this train, a column of 2,500 prisoners also came this way. Another 1,000 prisoners awaited transportation to the Bosque Redondo reservation. Carleton wrote to his superiors about the Navajo's condition: "The weather was very inclement, with terrible gales of wind and heavy falls of snow; the Indians were nearly naked; and, besides many died from dysentery."

Captain Francis McCabe left with about 800 prisoners from Fort Canby on March 20, 1864. At his disposal were only 23 wagons, hardly enough to adequately transport the prisoners. Rations amounting to one pound (0.4 kilograms) of meat or flour and a half-pound (0.2 kg) of bacon—meant to last for eight days—were soon consumed. The next day the People were forced to continue their march in a severe snowstorm that lasted four days. The officer refused to camp, to the great distress of the prisoners. Reaching Fort Wingate did not lead to improved conditions, as the army could only offer McCabe's party a half-pound of flour and a half-pound of beef for each captive. He also failed to receive additional clothing and transportation, both of which had been promised. Fearing a revolt, McCabe called in the headmen and assured them that full rations would be received at the next stop, Los Pinos, near Albuquerque. As the party traveled past the villages of Acoma and

Long Walk of the Navajo, 1864

Utah

Colorado

Oklahoma

Canyon de
Chelly *Navajo*

Chinle

**1868 TREATY
LANDS**

Ft. Defiance

Ft. Union

Santa Fe

Canadian R.

Kiowa

Las Vegas

Ft. Wingate

Albuquerque

Ft. Bascom

Ft. Sumner

New Mexico

**BOSQUE
REDONDO**

Arizona

Rio Grande

Ft. Stanton

Comanche

Pecos R.

Gila R.

Apache

Apache

●El Paso

Texas

N

MEXICO

Apache	Tribe
●	Non-Indian settlements
■	Forts
←	Long Walk

0   100 miles

0   100 km

© Infobase Learning

Note: Map shown with modern
boundaries.

This is a map of the Long Walk of the Navajo. More than 200 Navajo died
of cold and starvation on the grueling 300-mile trek (480 km) from Fort
Defiance to Bosque Redondo.

Laguna, a few Pueblo people tried to provide some assistance to
the captives. McCabe ordered his men to watch the columns to
make sure that no Navajo left with any Pueblo allies. Finally, the

caravan reached Los Pinos, where the captives rested for the next leg of the journey.

Upon their arrival at Fort Sumner, McCabe reported Navajo satisfaction and the promise of complete civilization, as cited in *Through White Men's Eyes*: "On getting sight of the reservation, with its ploughed and planted fields, its numerous acequias through which the water flowed and sparkled, and the green meadows on either side of the Pecos River, where horses, cattle, and sheep were quietly grazing, the Navajoes were greatly delighted and expressed great satisfaction with what they saw." Having left on April 24, the captives reached the Bosque Redondo on May 11. McCabe estimated that 110 had died while 25 had escaped.

By May 31, 1864, Captain H.B. Bristol reported that 5,174 Navajo were at the reservation. Of these, about a third were children and infants. By August, the number of captives swelled to 7,137. By November, at least 8,570 men, women, and children were interned at Hwéeldi (Bosque Redondo).

On September 9, 1866, Manuelito, who had surrendered at Fort Wingate, began the arduous journey to Hwéeldi. His band had dwindled from 500 to 23. Determined to make an example of this great leader, Carleton sent him through the outskirts of Santa Fe, intending to parade him before New Mexican citizens. The *Santa Fe Gazette* noted Manuelito's passing: "Manuelito and his band were brought to Santa Fe last week. They are to be taken to the Bosque Redondo Reservation and furnished a new home where they will have less of the cares of the State on their minds and more bread and meat to eat. Manuelito was the most stubborn of all the Navajo Chiefs and was the most difficult to be brought to terms."

The last large caravan of 417 prisoners was taken to the Bosque Redondo on December 13, 1866, when it left Fort Wingate. As this group approached the Rio Grande near Albuquerque, Carleton sent instructions to the commanding officer at the Albuquerque post: "I am afraid that the parties of Navajos who come in, and are sent by you from Albuquerque via Cañon Blanco to the Bosque

Redondo, will, at this season of the year, suffer for want of fuel and of shelter of bluffs and groves by that routing."

AT HWÉELDI

"Fair Carletonia" was far from what James Carleton had envisioned. The reality of life for the prisoners was deprivation, starvation, impoverishment, sickness and disease, death, and loneliness.

The Mescalero Apache, suffering from the cold and starving, arrived at the Bosque Redondo in early December 1862 and early January 1863. The Mescalero were expected to embrace American values of industry through farming and virtue through Christianity and western education. They were immediately instructed to build shelters for themselves. At the same time, the soldiers were busy constructing stables, warehouses, a hospital, and other necessary buildings. Expected to farm, by June, the Mescaleros had cleared, plowed, and planted more than 200 acres (80.9 ha) of corn, beans, and melons. They were expected to labor in the fields to cut the costs of their maintenance. Because few proper tools were available, the men used their hands to dig irrigation ditches. When Michael Steck, the New Mexico superintendent of Indian affairs, visited the reservation, he explained to Indian agent Lorenzo Labadie that his department could not furnish full rations and that the Mescalero should be allowed to hunt to supplement their rations. On one successful hunt, the Mescalero men bagged 86 antelopes. With the arrival of the Navajo prisoners in late 1863, the Apache had to compete for scarce resources with the more numerous Navajo.

The War and Indian departments feuded about who should be responsible for the prisoners, which compounded the difficulties at the reservation. When the first contingent of Navajo arrived at the fort, Steck, who was a steadfast critic of Carleton, ordered Labadie to refuse to take charge of the new arrivals. Steck pointed out the high cost of operating the Bosque Redondo and its unsuitable location, and argued that the Navajo population and their livestock overburdened the land base. Besides, added Steck, the

Apache and the Navajo were traditional enemies and hostilities would always exist between the two. He continually urged that the Navajo be settled in their own country.

In anticipation of the Navajo's arrival in late 1863, Carleton advertised for meat and foodstuffs in New Mexican newspapers. Some items he requested included shelled corn, with a delivery of 1,000 fanegas as early as December. (A fanega equaled 140 pounds, or 64 kilograms.) He also ordered additional shipments of shelled corn to be sent in January and March 1864. In the coming months, additional supplies would be ordered, including wheat meal, cornmeal, and heads of cattle and other livestock. Carleton was so determined that his program succeed that at times he ordered military commanders to reduce soldiers' rations—to ensure availability for the captives.

Because the captives arrived in the late fall of 1863 and in the early winter of 1864, there had been no time to prepare for spring planting. Relying on rations, Carleton ordered the fort commander to have the Navajo men prepare the land for planting. In addition, the work of digging irrigation ditches would keep them occupied. The Navajo agent reported with satisfaction that his charges had done an impressive job, digging miles of ditches. The women continued to weave at their looms, albeit under extremely stressful conditions. With access to little wool from their small flocks, the women added red bayeta cloth, which they unraveled and respun, and commercially prepared yarns. It is at this time that the transition in weaving began. Before this period, textiles had been woven for Navajo use and Navajo controlled the trade. By the end of the nineteenth century, non-Navajo traders began to dominate the trade and weavers saw little return for their labor. Two scholars, Paul Zolbrod and Roseann Willinks, interviewed a number of weavers who told stories about the textiles created during the time of Hwéeldi. They discovered that many of the weavers' creations reflected experiences at the Bosque Redondo reservation, including strong emotions of duress and hardship. Other textiles depicted the endeavors of Monster Slayer and Born for Water.

In the spring of 1864, Carleton was so enthusiastic about the state of his assimilation program that he reported that the Navajo and Mescalero were moving toward self-sufficiency; all was going as he had planned. In the latter part of the twentieth century, when American historians began to write Navajo history, many of them argued that the Navajo had benefited from their captivity at the Bosque Redondo, for they had acquired new technologies; replaced the digging stick with hoes, shovels, rakes, and plows; and learned about metalwork to make nails, horse and mule shoes, and, of course, jewelry. These historians marked the period as a time when the Navajo began the march on the path of progress and started to establish the modern Navajo Nation.

HOUSING CONDITIONS

In the hopes of changing Navajo living patterns, federal officials expected the captives to live in villages. The Navajo, pastoralists and farmers who lived in extended family networks, were accustomed to living miles from their neighbors. So, of course, they refused to live in such tight-knit quarters. Little attention was paid to providing them with adequate housing. In *Navajo Stories of the Long Walk*, Navajo storyteller Dugal Tsosie Begay said of the living conditions, "Most homes at Fort Sumner . . . were made by digging holes in the ground. Laid across the holes were logs and branches. On top of the logs and branches were piles of dirt." In contrast, the soldiers and officers lived more comfortably in barracks that had been built with adobe. Captives often had to walk miles, sometimes as far as 25 miles (40 km), to find enough wood to warm themselves and had so resorted to burning greasewood bushes.

The Navajo's refusal to live in shelters built next to one another was compounded by their beliefs about death and dead bodies. They would not enter any establishment where a person had died. Frustrated with the captives' avowal to follow their own rules,

Carleton finally agreed that families could abandon their shelter if a family member died and build a new shelter at the end of the row. The hospital, upon completion, had nine small rooms, with two of them used for a surgery and a kitchen. The hospital saw few patients, though, because the Navajo refused to enter any place where a person had died. In the spring of 1864, there were outbreaks of catarrh and dysentery. The Navajo and the Apache were constantly afflicted with various diseases, including pneumonia, typhoid, dysentery, pleurisy, skin problems like erysipelas, and rheumatism. Deadly epidemics of smallpox, measles, and cholera struck the post. For the Navajo, death became a daily occurrence and their population did not increase. In May 1864, the census showed that only three births had been reported.

The Navajo relied on their own medicine people and performed ceremonies such as the N'da, the Enemyway, as best as they could in such a foreign place. Dugal Tsosie Begay revealed that horses were not readily available and the N'da was performed using sticks for horses. Other ceremonies such as the Mountain Way chant and the Fire Dance continued to be performed to heal sicknesses. At the same time, many Navajo noted that their ceremonies and medicines could not heal the sicknesses and diseases that the whites had brought.

A FAILING PROGRAM

The inadequacies of the "civilizing program" were evident in multiple ways. Rations were always inadequate and of inferior quality. In April 1864, the Navajo prisoners were receiving two and a half pounds of meat and two and a half pounds (1.1 kg) of flour every fifth day. The starving men, women, and children ate their portions in two days, leaving them to suffer miserably until the next issuance of rations. As cited in *The Army and the Navajo*, Labadie reported, "They eat their rations in two days, and during the other three days they suffer, eating hides, and begging wherever they can." In his recollections in *Navajo Stories*, Howard W. Gorman said of the Navajo people's constant hunger, "The prisoners begged the Army for some corn, and the leaders also pleaded for it for their people." In desperation, boys wandered off to where the mules and horses were corralled and poked around in the manure to take undigested corn out of it. The kernels were roasted in hot ashes and eaten.

Carleton came under fire for awarding contracts to his supporters, who profited enormously from selling supplies and food for the Bosque Redondo. Carleton's supporters argued that the cost of buying supplies, including beef, was good for New Mexico's economy. Labadie, though, reported that the flour provided to the Mescalero was unfit for consumption. The contractor William H. Moore, a prominent New Mexican and a mining speculator, had sold flour with bits of slate, broken dried bread, and a mixture that looked like plaster of paris in it. Other supplies coming into the reservation were reported to be of "livid quality."

At times, the captives' rations were cut in half. Gerald Thompson has calculated that the daily issuance of food added up to 1,000 calories, totally inadequate and essentially starvation rations. To control access to food supplies, army personnel devised methods to ensure that each person received his or her meager share. For example, because the soldiers feared that some Navajo were drawing more than one ration, they created metal ration discs to be exchanged for food. The desperate captives soon learned to create replicas of the discs.

Casting about for ways to supplement the food supply, the Navajo agent authorized the Navajo men to hunt wild game. At another time, when supplies were late, Carleton considered ways to stretch the food, including the construction of ovens to bake loaves of bread. Among the captives were headmen and their families, who brought sizable herds of cattle, sheep, and goats. In several cases, the army purchased their livestock, which went toward the rations. Several times the supplies were threatened when freights met up with Native men, including Navajo, who attacked them and sometimes made off with their booty. In one attack, the Navajo men ambushed the incoming freight and made off with 5,200 sheep and 13 horses and burros. In this case, the army, aided by the Mescalero, followed them and recovered most of the sheep and provisions.

Times were so desperate that some women were forced into prostitution in exchange for food. Girls as young as 12 and 13 sold their bodies for a pint of cornmeal from the soldiers. The rise in venereal diseases, particularly syphilis, quickly surpassed malnutrition as the most pressing health problem on the reservation. Blaming the Navajo women, federal officials declared that their "loose morals" were the cause of the disease running rampant throughout the fort. To combat the problem, Carleton ordered that women who lived with soldiers, reported to be "laundresses" and "housekeepers," would no longer receive rations. In contrast, agent Labadie said that reports of Mescalero women selling their bodies were almost nonexistent. Federal officials surmised that the Mescalero women did not engage in prostitution because of severe penalties, including having the tips of their noses cut off. The captives lived in such extreme conditions that they acted in ways they normally would not have in order to survive. Further, as feminist scholar Andrea Smith has pointed out, the conquest of America has included the sexual violation of Native women.

In sum, the first year at the Bosque Redondo was not as rosy as Carleton had reported to his superiors. The first six months saw serious setbacks, including destroyed harvests, inadequate supplies and rations, low birthrates, and reports that Navajo were attacking New Mexican settlements. On Christmas Eve, 7,800 Navajo were counted to receive distributions of blankets, bolts of cloth, awls, buttons and beads, sheep shears, scissors, knives, hoes, shovels, and axes. Of the first year at the reservation, Gerald Thompson observed of the condition of the Navajo, "It was clear that many Navajos would be buried that winter, in the cold strange Pecos country, for want of food and clothing."

On May 1, 1864, the first desertions were reported. Forty-three Navajo disappeared from the reservation, and on April 30, 1865, another 900 captives escaped. In the darkness of night, on June 14, Navajo leaders Ganado Blanco and Barboncito and about 500 of their bands fled the reservation. Carleton sent the army out in hopes of intercepting them. Frustrated at the number of Navajo leaving the reservation, Carleton issued an order: Navajos caught outside of the boundaries without a pass were to be punished. When one Navajo man was apprehended 25 miles (40 km) southeast of Las Vegas and returned to the fort, he was forced to wear a heavy ball and chain for the next two months and put to hard labor.

One April night in 1865, the Apache leader Ojo Blanco fled the reservation with 42 of his band. By May, as problems weighed down the operation of the reservation, the rest of the Mescalero left in the darkness to return to their homeland. They executed a brilliant plan in which they broke into several small groups and scattered into several directions. Unable to decide which group to chase, the army admitted failure and returned to the post without their victims. In May 1865, it was reported that more than 1,000 Navajo were absent from the reservation. At the same time, captives were still arriving from Navajo country. By 1867, more and more captives were reported missing from the reservation. Sometimes the soldiers were sent to look for the fleeing Navajo; others escaped with little notice. Returning to their homeland was fraught with danger, however, for the freedom runners faced many risks, including an unfamiliar landscape and slave raiders.

Amid growing public criticism, Carleton hastened to assure his superiors that the reservation was indeed succeeding. Living in Santa Fe, Carleton sent his orders: The irrigation ditches must be extended and individual Navajo families should have land allocated to them along the ditches. As cited in *The Army and the Navajo*, he went on to write, "The garrison at Sumner must realize the value of the overall program both to the Indians and to civilization, and give a hand in plowing, planting, and enlarging the ditches." In reality, however, the reservation was so overburdened with the costs of maintenance that Carleton told the commanders at forts Defiance and Wingate to keep the prisoners waiting to make the journey to Hwéeldi. By April 1865, 9,026 Natives, the majority being Navajo, were at the reservation.

THE BEGINNING OF THE END

In June 1865, the Doolittle Commission reached New Mexico to investigate conditions at the reservation and the treatment of Natives by civil and military authorities. Spurred by reports of corruption in the Indian Service, Senator James Doolittle headed an investigation into the conditions at Fort Sumner. The final report, known as the Doolittle Report, was published in January 1867 and acknowledged that the Navajo had not improved their lives at the reservation. While the response to the report did little to address the suffering of the captives, the report did pave the way for the People's eventual return to their homeland.

By 1866 Carleton was relieved of his command in New Mexico. "Fair Carletonia" was to be the casualty of sustained public criticism, mismanagement, and season after season of harsh climate. Captives continually longing for their homeland were also an important factor in the failure of Carleton's grand scheme. Whenever federal officials visited the fort, Navajo men and women pleaded to be allowed to return to their homeland. Navajo stories indicated that they often took matters into their own hands and acted to ensure their survival. Many stories tell how the medicine people conducted a ceremony, Ma'ii' Bizéé'nast'á (Put Bead in Coyote's Mouth), to prophesize about their future as a people. According to Fred Descheene in *Navajo Stories*, the ancestors said, "We are lonesome for our land. How can we return to it?" Longing for their homeland, the medicine men conducted Ma'ii' Bizéé'nast'á by capturing a coyote and placing a bead in its mouth. The medicine men interpreted the coyote's actions: The People would return to Diné Bekéyah before too long.

The Navajo were losing heart and threatened rebellion. In August 1867, a fight broke out between the Navajo men and the army soldiers. According to Navajo leaders, a misunderstanding between Navajo warriors and the soldiers led to bloodshed when the Navajo thought the soldiers meant to fight them. The matter was resolved peacefully, but it was only one of several that occurred at the reservation. In the spring of 1868, federal officials finally conceded that the Bosque Redondo reservation had failed.

On May 28, 1868, General William T. Sherman and Samuel Tappan met with Navajo leaders to discuss the condition of the Navajo. A council convened and Barboncito acted as the Navajo's chief negotiator. Barboncito described the harsh realities of life at the reservation and his people's hopes for a future of peace and prosperity. Of their impoverishment, according to *The Navajo Treaty–1868*, he said, "I cannot rest comfortable at night. I am ashamed to go to the Commissary for my food, it looks as if somebody was waiting to give it to me." The leader asserted, "Our Grandfathers had no idea of living in any other country except our own. It was told to us by our forefathers, that we were never to move east of the Rio Grande or west of the San Juan rivers and I think that our coming here has been the cause of so much death among us and our animals." He explained that they had endeavored to make the best of their situation but the land did not know them: "This ground we were brought here we have done all we could possibly do, but found it to be labor in vain, and have therefore quit it. For that reason we have not planted or tried to do anything this year."

General Sherman said that he was persuaded by the Navajo leader's words and added, "You are right, the world is big enough for all the people it contains and all should live at peace with their neighbors." The general suggested the possibility of removing the Navajo to Indian Territory. Barboncito's reply was firm: "I hope to God you will not ask me to go to any other country except my own." Sherman agreed to allow the Navajo to return to their land. With the proceedings ending well for the Navajo, a thankful Barboncito declared, "After we get back to our country, it will

Barboncito is photographed circa 1870. The Navajo chief convinced General William Sherman to move the Navajo back to their native lands.

Treaty of 1868 (Naal Tsoos Sání)

On June 1, 1868, Navajo leaders signed what would be the last treaty with the United States. They called it Naal Tsoos Sání, or "Old Paper." The treaty remains an important document that symbolizes Navajo sovereignty and reflects the nation-to-nation relationship that Navajo leaders have with the American government. Over the decades, the Navajo have celebrated the signing of the treaty to remind their citizens about the trust relationship between the Navajo Nation and the United States and to proclaim and recognize the imperative to become a fully sovereign nation with distinctive cultural values and teachings.

In 1968, in recognition of the treaty, Navajo Tribal Chairman Raymond Nakai proclaimed a centennial, and throughout the year, cultural events, including a reenactment of the Long Walk and the signing of the treaty, provided Navajo citizens time and space to think about the 100 years since their ancestors returned from the Hwéeldi prison.

In 1998, the Friends of the Navajo Treaty Project, under the direction of Navajo scholars Evangeline Parsons-Yazzie and Joe Kee, brought the original treaty from the National Archives in Washington, D.C., for a yearlong display at Northern Arizona University. Thousands of Navajo and their allies traveled to the university in Flagstaff to view the sacred document. Naal Tsoos Sání was exhibited alongside photographs and material culture to show what Navajo life was like at Hwéeldi in the 1860s. The exhibition served as a marker to remember the collective experiences of their ancestors. The treaty allowed them

brighten up again and Navajos will be as happy as the land. Black clouds will rise and there will be plenty of rain. Corn will grow in abundance and everything will look happy." On May 30, the council ended and the treaty was drawn up.

moments to send prayers to the Holy People, their ancestors, and their leaders who had shed their blood to keep their land and their freedom. On June 1, 1999, the Friends of the Treaty Project celebrated Navajo sovereignty with daylong events. The farewell to the treaty honored the Navajo who had survived Hwéeldi and called for the Navajo to continue to work for the sovereignty of their Nation.

In 1992, the New Mexico legislature passed a bill requesting that the Office of Cultural Affairs continue efforts to establish the Bosque Redondo as a memorial to the Navajo people. The Office of Cultural Affairs worked with the Navajo Nation to offer interpretations that incorporated the Navajo perspective on this historical landmark. Many people realized that the Navajo often had different and even contradictory perspectives on the meaning of the Long Walk and Hwéeldi. For the Navajo, the memorial should honor and preserve the memories of their ancestors who transmitted their traumatic experiences of Hwéeldi through oral tradition. For others, the memorial should acknowledge the injustices perpetuated on the Navajo by the United States. On June 4, 2005, the Bosque Redondo Memorial was officially opened, with invited speakers offering interpretations of the meaning of the place. Not surprisingly, most of the audience was Navajo. The Bosque Redondo Memorial is a place that calls up the violence of federal Indian policy on Native peoples and the Navajo and, at the same time, it honors the courage, resilience, and vision of the Navajo ancestors. Today, Navajo visitors to the Bosque Redondo Memorial are a common sight and the staff works hard to accommodate them.

The treaty was signed on June 1, 1868. Barboncito and Manuelito were among the signatories. The Navajo leaders agreed to a reservation carved out of their original territory; the new reservation was about a quarter of the territory they had formerly claimed. They also agreed to an American education for their children and instructions in Christianity for their people. The federal government would provide annuities for 10 years, which was supposed to be enough support until the Navajo gained self-sufficiency. The Navajo were not to object to the establishment of trading posts on their reservation. Years later, the People would remember the words Manuelito spoke at Hwéeldi about the importance of 'Iiná, or Life. He had said, "Life does not end. It goes on." The treaty reminds the Navajo of how their leaders had been willing to lay down their lives if it meant that their people would have the land. They remember their grandmothers' and grandfathers' courage in the face of American colonialism. Foremost, the Treaty of 1868 affirms the sovereignty of the Navajo Nation.

Seventeen days later, on June 18, more than 8,000 Navajo began the journey home. The caravan extended for at least 10 miles (16 km). Fifty-six wagons carried the elders, the ill, and the young. Although they had only 940 sheep, 1,025 goats, and 1,550 horses among them, it would not be long before their herds would prosper. Once they passed Albuquerque and crossed the Rio Grande, they recognized their sacred Tsoodził (Mount Taylor) and cried with joy and thanked the Holy People for answering their prayers. They were almost home. About their journey back, Manuelito said, "The days and nights were long before it came time for us to go to our homes. . . . When we saw the top of the mountain from Albuquerque we wondered if it was our mountain, and we felt like talking to the ground, we loved it so, and some of the old men and women cried with joy when they reached their homes."

Today, the People remember their ancestors' ordeals under American expansion. They honor their leaders for being warriors who tried to protect the land and the people. The stories of this period provide space to think about the U.S. government's treatment of its indigenous peoples, for the United States has yet to shoulder its responsibility to act justly and humanely. The next chapter examines how the Navajo reestablished their lives once they were back in Diné Bekéyah.

The Era of
Livestock Reduction
and Beyond

The early reservation period up to the 1880s is often depicted as a time of relative prosperity for the Navajo. Indian agents, however, worried about an impending crisis if the federal government did not heed their reports of denuded land and environmental deterioration. In the 1930s, the Navajo saw yet another transition in their lives, one that would have drastic consequences, for they saw their economy devastated, which affected all other sectors of their communities. Newly appointed Indian Affairs commissioner John Collier carried out the federal government's response to the environmental crisis—reducing Navajo livestock by 50 percent. Although Collier's administration is often seen as a new era in Native American history, the Navajo do not have positive things to say about Collier, as he is forever associated with livestock reduction. Collier's policies rendered the Navajo dependent on outside sources, including the federal government and an external market.

In the end, livestock reduction did not bring about the changes that Collier envisioned for the Navajo, and scholars have looked back to this time and asked about the reasons for the environmental deterioration and whether there might have been better ways to address the crisis. For the Navajo, forced livestock reduction caused much grief, shock, and outrage and is seen in the same light as the Long Walk. This chapter explores how the environmental crisis affected the Navajo and their economy, which was based upon raising livestock. Navajo responses to livestock reduction included the transition to a wage economy, the beginnings of a modern Navajo government, and the introduction of the peyote religion. Education also saw some changes as cultural pluralism become a model in Navajo country.

INCREASING FLOCKS

In the early reservation period, agents of the Bureau of Indian Affairs (BIA) had encouraged the Navajo to increase their flocks, but by the 1930s, their flocks had reached the one million mark. For decades Indian agents had tried to deal with the issue of increasing flocks on a limited land base that was checked by non-Indian settlers who refused to allow Navajo herders access to pasture lands. Indian agents asked for appropriations from Congress to improve water sources and buy land for Navajo use. They submitted reports to the BIA detailing the effects of overgrazing on the Navajo reservation and warned that only drastic steps would reverse the environmental damage. In the 1920s, Indian agents tried to enact a number of solutions, including eradicating sheep scabies; reducing the number of horses, which were seen as worthless; and introducing better-quality sheep. Their efforts were based upon scientific methods for producing livestock for the market.

The Navajo were reluctant to cut back on their herds and understood the reasons for the denuded lands differently from white officials. For example, an accumulation of sheep and goats reflected the status of a family and the individual. The ability to establish vast

The Navajos' success at sheepherding led to overgrazing and denuded land. In an attempt to correct the situation, the U.S. government imposed the extermination of 50 percent of the reservation's livestock population.

herds indicated that a person had characteristics such as humility, compassion, and generosity. Learning how to care for livestock also shaped one to be thrifty, hardworking, and responsible. Foremost, livestock ownership indicated that one had attended to proper ceremonies and rituals. Only when a person had conducted the proper prayers to attain these animals did the Holy People comply.

Foresters William Zeh in 1930 and E.A. Johnson in 1931 described the overgrazed condition of the land. Zeh described trampled and denuded lands around water holes and hogans, cropped juniper trees and yellow pine trees from goats, a growing scarcity of grasses, and increasing soil erosion. Summer flash floods had washed away sections of stream banks so that wide, deep gullies cut across vast swaths of land. Commending the efforts to expand the reservation, Zeh urged the elimination of horses, suggested improved breeds of sheep and goats along with the gradual reduction of goats, and stressed the need for permanent stockwater. He also suggested a program of rodent control, the elimination of prairie dogs, and a project to introduce the Navajo to better methods of stock handling. Johnson reported that, everywhere he traveled, the land was bare of grasses and that there was only a fraction of forage that had been normally present in these places. Johnson calculated that the reservation was overstocked by 50 percent, including thousands of horses. He expressed doubt that Navajo herders would voluntarily regulate range use or limit stock. Johnson urged attention to the crisis, no matter Navajo reaction.

THE GOVERNMENT'S RESPONSE

After several decades of little action and few appropriations to address the problem, federal officials finally responded. In particular, scholars have recently charged that federal officials finally paid attention to the impending crisis because conditions on the Navajo reservation were causing silting at Boulder Dam. The time for action was to fall to John Collier, the newly appointed Indian Affairs commissioner in 1933. Despite Navajo opnion, Collier's administration has often been regarded as a positive era in federal-Indian relations because he introduced legislation that reversed decades of policies that had decimated Native cultures and languages.

Formerly a social worker, Collier came to the Southwest, visited Pueblo communities, and identified Native ways of life as sources for rejuvenating what ailed America. During this time, many Americans felt a sense of alienation and loss, for it seemed that their society lacked spirituality and an appreciation of nature. Seeing some worth in Native cultural thought and practices, Collier recognized the importance of land to Native peoples, and through legislation, he ended land allotment, which had broken up Native lands and opened them up to white settlement. Collier sought to preserve tribal cultural traditions and languages and instigated education curriculums that reflected his philosophy of cultural pluralism. He authored legislation to establish tribal governments based upon the best of American democracy.

In 1933, before the Navajo Tribal Council, Collier laid out his plan to recover the land and preserve tribal traditions: It included expanding reservation boundaries, developing new water sources, embracing scientific management practices, and creating a centralized administrative center under a single superintendent. His efforts were also intended to address the national concern over soil erosion, concern over silt runoff into Boulder Dam, and the plummeting price for wool. Collier tried to assure the tribal council that he would not force the Navajo to reduce their flocks. According to Marsha Weisiger's *Dreaming of Sheep in Navajo Country*, he said, "As long as I am commissioner, we are not going to use compulsion on the Navajo tribe." He complimented the tribe for being a model of self-reliance and self-government.

From 1933 to 1937, livestock reduction was enacted. The first reduction called for the Navajo to decrease their herds by 100,000 head and required stockholders to reduce their flocks by 10 percent across the board. For this first reduction, the Navajo were generally willing to get rid of some of their flocks, particularly gummers or aging sheep, which even the traders would not buy. In one month, Indian agents bought 86,500 sheep and filled the holding pens in Gallup. These sheep were destined for canneries back east. They would be meat for the needy. On the other hand, some Navajo were opposed and voiced concern that the tribal council did not represent their views. They said that they were being reduced to poverty. In particular, the women who owned large herds resented the idea that a handful of men should tell them what to do.

This reduction was largely unsuccessful because large stock-holders culled unproductive head while small operators were reduced to destitution because they had to get rid of their prime stock. Again, Collier went to the tribal council, mandating siz-able reductions: 150,000 head of grown stock, of which 100,000 were to be goats. Because goats moved quickly, it was thought that they were the most responsible for trampling the land. Collier also called for the sale of at least 80 percent of the lamb crop every year and the castration of billy goats. The Navajo were assured that they would not go hungry, for money from New Deal programs was available and they would find wage jobs on erosion-control proj-ects. Collier also promised more land if the Navajo would comply with his program. Two congressional bills had been drawn up to purchase land in Arizona and New Mexico. While the tribal coun-cil seemed to endorse Collier's plans, the people were a different story. In Crownpoint, New Mexico, when the tribal council met, 500 to 600 Navajo men and women appeared. They demanded to know what they were supposed to do when their livestock was taken. The older people said that they were too old to work for wages. They depended on their animals for food and clothing.

William Zeh was charged with reducing the number of goats in 1934. Zeh felt that, if the Navajo were exposed to scientific man-agement knowledge, they would agree that reduction was for the best. In 1934, the U.S. secretary of agriculture purchased 150,000 goats, or half of the Navajo holdings, and up to 50,000 sheep at $1 a head. In the summer and fall of 1934, livestock were rounded up for sale in the eastern markets. The long distances and arid conditions, however, proved too much for their transport. In one case, Zeh arranged for goats to be bought and taken to market. The cannery in Phoenix, though, could handle only a fraction of the numbers slated for the market. Zeh was determined to carry out the reduction, regardless of the problems. In the western part of the reservation, 7,500 goats and nearly 3,400 sheep were purchased and then shot en masse and left to rot. These acts were gross violations to the Navajo people, who thought of the livestock as the foundation of their lives. Alk'inanibaa' Burbank, who lived in the Lukachukai area, recalled that the people were afraid of what was happening, but that they were also afraid to speak up or act because they knew the capacity of the federal government to use force on them. They remembered the violence their ancestors had endured under American rule in the 1860s.

At the beginning of 1935, the reduction program was in shambles. The third reduction was intended to be "voluntary" and was a failure. The plan to purchase livestock resulted in the sale of only 13,312 goats and 13,866 sheep; Collier had hoped for 250,000 head. The Navajo resisted so much that Collier refused to convene the tribal council because of the objections. At times, Collier made promises such as land extensions, improved stock water, and wage work through New Deal programs; however. these promises were tied to livestock reduction. According to data collected in 1936, sheep and goats were down by 35.5 percent from 1930, but more than 80 percent of the reservation remained overgrazed and depleted. In early 1934, Congress added about a million acres to the Navajo reservation, but Collier was unable to come through on his promise of additional land in New Mexico because of non-Indian opposition.

NEW LEADERS

One Navajo leader who emerged during this period was Jacob Morgan. As a child Morgan was among the first generation to go away for an education. His mother had died, and during his time at boarding school, his father also passed away. After attending a school in Grand Junction, Colorado, he went on to Hampton Institute in Virginia. Years later, he returned to his homeland a devout Christian and eventually became a missionary. Morgan entered the fray over livestock reduction and was a formidable opponent of Collier's policies. His vocal opposition eventually led to his being elected chairman of the tribe in 1938. Although Morgan opposed Collier's plans, he also questioned the need for more land and advocated a return to agriculture as a means for making a living.

From 1935 to 1940, Navajo livestock was reduced by more than a third. By 1940, the Navajo were openly resisting the reduction. People in Shiprock, New Mexico, were told to bring their horses in for branding. Protesters urged noncompliance. On January 22, 1940, warrants were issued for the arrests of Fred Begay, Kitty Blackhorse, Shorthair Begay, Frank Todecheeny, Clizzie Clonie Bega, and Delewoshie. Appearing before a judge, they were ordered to comply with the regulations. Kitty Blackhorse answered the judge by throwing his jacket onto the floor and sitting down. According to Peter Iverson's *Diné*, he said, "I don't want to hear what you have to say, but sentence me right now." Blackhorse's three sons came to support their father and sat beside him. There was quite a bit of commotion before things quieted down and those arrested made their way home. The next day, they returned and refused to be jailed. A crowd grew around them, and federal officials decided it was best to postpone arrests.

In 1941, the federal government's issuance of temporary permits for stock signaled the end of livestock reduction. The coming of World War II diverted attention away from events in Navajo country.

Ultimately, Collier's ambitions to save the Navajo from themselves and to restore the land to its former capacity met with failure. Rather, livestock reduction led to impoverishment, and the Navajo had to find another means of support. The land continued to need restoration. Collier's declaration that he would not force compliance was false, and he failed to fulfill his promise of additional lands because of powerful non-Indian political influences. The Navajo came to despise him, and when he presented them with plans to change their government based upon the Indian Reorganization Act, the Navajo people narrowly defeated the measure. The vote against the act was a severe blow to Collier, who believed that he had acted in the best interests of the Navajo.

NAVAJO AND HOPI LAND DISPUTE

Another legacy of livestock reduction was the carving of the land into range management districts and the issuance of livestock permits. Chapters, the local community political unit, also date from this era. Based upon Indian agent Francis Leupp's use of the chapter concept to get local input and decisions, Collier implemented chapters throughout Navajoland. Although once the chapter meetings became hotbeds of dissent and opposition to reduction, Collier quickly banned the meetings. When the land was divided into 18 districts for centralized management, the Hopi—who also were coping with the environmental crisis—were placed in a single district, District 6. The designation of District 6 as exclusive for Hopi occupancy again raised questions about the rightful owners of the reservation. Ultimately, when federal officials turned their attention to the question of rightful ownership, the Navajo suffered another removal and relocation, the effects of which are ongoing.

Although the creation of the 1882 Hopi reservation (surrounded by Navajo lands) through executive order is depicted as the beginning of relationships between the two tribes, there is a longer history. In 1918, Indian agent Leo Crane wrote to his superiors and included a history of Indian agents who had reported on the state of affairs between the Navajo and the Hopi, dating from 1850. His history offers a window into the relationship between the two tribes and Indian agents' efforts to deal with Navajo-Hopi relationships and occupancy of the land. Both tribal peoples farmed in washes and traveled across the region for various purposes. Indian agents reported the numbers of Hopi living in their villages and claimed that they lived in fear of the Navajo. At other times Indian agents noted friendly relations between the tribes. In 1888, Navajo agent S.S. Patterson reported Hopi complaints about Navajo thefts of their horses and other problems. In 1902, the Keams Canyon Agency was established to administer Hopi lands and the surrounding lands of the 1882 reservation occupied by the Navajo. Inspector H.S. Traylor investigated Hopi complaints and surmised that the Navajo invaded Hopi space because of Hopi cowardliness. Traylor's portrayal of the Hopi as passive, fearful people who wanted only to live in peace was often presented in juxtaposition to the portrayal of Navajo as aggressive raiders who caused conflict with their neighbors all the time. These stereotypes of both tribes would be drawn upon by federal officials and then attorneys involved in the legal cases of the land dispute.

In 1926, federal officials were hopeful that the Hopi were finally seeing the wisdom in coming down from the mesas and engaging in cattle raising and expanding their cornfields. In 1927 commissioner of Indian Affairs Charles H. Burke responded to recommendations by federal officials that Indians living in the northwest part of the Hopi reservation be placed under the jurisdiction of the Western Navajo Agency, which was based in Tuba City, rather than under the Keams Canyon Agency. The shift in administrative center would make supervision easier. Tom Pavatea, a Hopi, worried that placing the administration of Hopi affairs under a Navajo agency could mean the loss of Hopi land. Burke assured him that the move was meant only to expedite federal business for the Indians.

Crane noted that, in 68 years, federal officials had failed to address the issue of the rightful occupancy of the lands. He suggested that the Navajo be removed but also admitted that removing Navajo north and south of the Hopi mesas would require the government to ensure an adequate water supply for the Navajo. He also recommended a boundary to designate Hopi land. Of the dispute between the Navajo and the Hopi, historian Richard Clemmer remarked, "Navajos had begun to get the upper hand in the competition for land." Navajo population had increased so that they "accounted for nearly 45% of the population of the 1882 Reservation." With the expansion of Navajo, Hopi, and Mormons in the western region of the Navajo and Hopi reservations, "there was no room for anybody to expand there." The creation of District 6 for exclusive Hopi occupancy became the first official federal policy to segregate the Navajo and Hopi. The boundaries of District 6 were finalized on April 24, 1943, and included the 650,013 acres that became the Hopi reservation in 1962.

In general, federal officials had paid little attention to the affairs of the Navajo and the Hopi in a remote area of Arizona. When valuable natural resources were discovered, however, it became necessary to clarify rightful ownership of the land and, hence, mineral resources. In 1958, Congress passed Public Law 85-547, authorizing the Navajo and Hopi tribes to proceed to a legal suit, *Healing v. Jones*, to determine each tribe's rights to the 1882 reservation outside of District 6. In 1962, a three-judge panel of the U.S. District Court of Arizona issued its decision in the suit between the two tribes. The court acknowledged Navajo occupancy of the 1882 reservation in "Indian fashion," long before the creation of the reservation. The court's findings also noted that about 300 Navajo had been settled in the 1882 reservation legally by the action of the secretary of the interior from 1909 to 1911, while tribal settlement was accomplished by secretarial actions from 1931 to 1943. The court determined that the Hopi Tribe, subject to the trust title of the United States, "has the exclusive right and interest, both as to the surface and subsurface, including all resources" to District 6. The court also found that the Hopi and Navajo tribes, subject to the trust title of the United States, "have joint undivided and equal rights and interest both as to the surface and subsurface, including all resources" to the 1882 area outside of District 6.

In 1974, lawmakers in Washington, D.C., passed Public Law 93-531, the Navajo-Hopi Land Settlement Act. This act partitioned the 1882 reservation equally between the Navajo and the Hopi. This area soon became known as the Joint Use Area (JUA).

In 1933, Navajo Chief Chee Dodge (*far left*) met with commissioner of Indian Affairs John Collier (*second from left*). Their sons, Assistant Commissioner Charles Collier (*second from right*), and Tom Dodge (*far right*), chairman of the Navajo Tribal Council, posed with them for this photograph.

In 1977, U.S. District Judge John Walsh divided the surface estate equally between the two tribes. Those who lived on the side awarded to the other tribe were served notice to vacate. About 12,000 Navajo and 160 Hopi found themselves on the wrong side of the boundary.

After nearly 40 years and several deadlines to finalize relocation have passed, a handful of Navajo remain on lands awarded to the Hopi. These resisters reside at Big Mountain, which is said to sit atop a rich deposit of coal. To date, U.S. taxpayers have paid more than $500 million to relocate the Navajo. The cost of administering the settlement of the dispute was wildly underesti-mated. Also unexpected was the depth of the Navajo's determina-tion to challenge the law to relocate them.

Significantly, women have been at the forefront of the resis-tance to relocation. These matriarchs come from generations of grandmothers and mothers who claimed the privilege of dictating land use. Over decades, the oldest generation of resisters has aged and some have died, but their vows to remain are remembered. In November 1999, Jenny Manybeads, age 115, passed away. She had been the plaintiff in a lawsuit, *Manybeads v. United States*, which charged that the United States had violated her freedom of religion when it ordered her and other Navajo removed from their home-land. In 2001, the U.S. Supreme Court refused to hear the case. On April 23, 2002, another matriarch who refused to be relocated, Roberta Blackgoat, died. Blackgoat spent 40 years of her life as a staunch resister to relocation. She articulated the passion of the Navajo who refused to move away. At one point she said, "Many of us will die before we allow the profaning of what we know to be good, just, and holy. The Creator is the only one who is going to relocate us."

As scholars have noted, the question of mineral rights has been central to the conflict over the rightful owner of the 1882 reservation, for only then could the coal and water resources be developed. As David Brugge has asserted, "As long as conflicts over land involved only the Indians themselves, the powers that were in Washington found little reason to give a search for a more comprehensive solution very high priority." For the Navajo, evic-tion from the Hopi partition land has meant relocation to urban off-reservation sites, to chapters on the reservation where there is already a land squeeze, and to lands bought for their occupancy and formally established as the 110th chapter on the Navajo Nation in Sanders, Arizona. Because of this, relocation has resulted in a profound sense of alienation and loss. The Navajo cultural prac-tices and traditions have suffered, and there has been considerable language erosion. Another response to the forced relocation has come with the Navajo asking the United Nations to investigate the U.S. policy of removal as an act of genocide.

RETHINKING LIVESTOCK REDUCTION

The Navajo-Hopi land dispute is but one issue that has roots in the events of the livestock reduction. Today, historians and other scholars revisit the reductions with questions about how the reductions were conducted and how federal officials placed the blame for environmental degradation directly on Navajo livestock. These scholars argue that federal officials failed to understand the depth and scope of the Navajo people's attachment to their livestock. Destroying their animals showed the ultimate disrespect to the Navajo people. Government authorities also disparaged Navajo knowledge about nature, land, and their livestock, and refused to listen to the Navajo about how to implement livestock reduction. Rather, says historian Peter Iverson, "Had Collier been astute enough to take advantage of this fleeting opportunity for genuine cooperation and a significant degree of self-determination, the course of livestock reduction might have been quite different."

It can only remain a source of conjecture to wonder how the Navajo themselves might have handled the problem of overgrazing and its effect on their land, for they recognized the problem. As Richard White has observed, the problem was not that there were too many Navajo and livestock, but that scarce resources had been unevenly distributed to benefit non-Indians. From 1860 to 1930, the Navajo population quadrupled, rising from 10,000 to 40,000 people. In the same period, the non-Indian population in Arizona grew from 6,482 to 435,573, while New Mexico's non-Indian population grew from 61,547 to 423,317. No one argued that non-Indians had a problem of overpopulation. Thus, the crisis of the environmental conditions on the reservation was directly related to the Navajo's diminished access to lands off the reservation and the redistribution of scarce resources.

More recently, historian Marsha Weisiger has argued that Collier and other federal Indian officials made matters worse when they antagonized the Navajo and refused to listen to and involve them in decision making concerning the environmental crisis. She asserts that Collier's mistakes in ignoring the importance of long-estab-lished cultural patterns, the disparagement of local knowledge and cultural understandings of nature, and the refusal to include Navajo at the top administrative levels led to Navajo distrust of the federal government, which continues today. Further, Weisiger notes that, if Navajo women had been involved in the decision making then livestock reduction might have happened with more cooperation.

Another reassessment of how and when the Navajo live-stock reduction was instigated considers how livestock reduction was enforced once it was thought that the economy of the larger Southwest was threatened by conditions on the Navajo reserva-tion. This reassessment also reconsiders the assumptions of the day that put the blame for the overgrazed conditions directly on Navajo flocks. At the same time that overgrazing was taking a toll on the land, there was also a long period of drought followed by intense summer rains that initiated the deep gullying, which fur-ther destroyed grazing and farm lands. According to tree-ring data, the 1870s and 1880s were extremely dry, although there were some years of rain. In 1899 and 1904, there was again severe drought with little snow and rainfall. From 1905 to 1920, sudden thunderstorms further added to the erosion, gullying, and loss of topsoil.

TRANSITIONS—EDUCATION, RELIGION, AND THE WAGE ECONOMY

Navajo responses to livestock reduction were many and varied. One area that has received considerable attention is John Collier's policies regarding Indian education reform and how those reforms reshaped Navajo education. As noted earlier, Navajo children did not attend American schools in large numbers. Navajo isolation in far-flung residences and the lack of funds to enforce the Treaty of 1868 probably added to the inattention to the children's educa-tion. Navajo resistance also contributed to low numbers of chil-dren enrolled in schools on and off the reservation. Under Collier's policy of cultural pluralism, however, day schools were established, and these schools added aspects of Navajo culture to their curriculums. For example, in the 1940s, Navajo children read from Ann Nolan Clark's readers about Navajo life. Military style discipline and training were replaced with classes in weaving and silversmithing. Teachers assigned topics such as how to make Navajo foods and how to care for livestock. They encouraged children to share stories based upon their cultural values. The Navajo Service, a branch of the Bureau of Indian Affairs, encouraged parents to come to the schools and turned schools into community centers where parents could learn about car repair and sewing, among other activities.

Another development that scholars have documented is the introduction of the peyote religion during this time. Traumatized by the loss of their sheep, goats, and horses, some Navajo turned to the peyote religion for healing and inspiration. They were introduced to the peyote way by their Ute neighbors in the northern region of Navajo country. Perhaps one reason that the new religion was attractive was because it was less elaborate than the traditional ceremonies, which lasted for 10 days in some cases and required a huge number of livestock. Livestock was used to pay the medicine person, was given away during portions of the ceremonies, and was a source of food for the hundreds of relatives who came to support the hosts. With the loss of their livestock, Navajo families found the costs of the more elaborate ceremonies prohibitive. One ceremony could wipe out a family's entire livestock holdings.

In contrast to the more elaborate traditional ceremonies, the peyote religion required one night of prayer. Collier, who advocated tolerance toward Native religions, was receptive to the new religion that was quickly gaining members on Navajo land. The Navajo Tribal Council and traditionalists, however, did not like the new religion and considered it too foreign. Tribal council members moved to make it illegal to sell, use, or possess the peyote cactus, a psychoactive plant that was at the center of the prayer meetings. The peyote plant originated in Mexico, where its healing qualities had been known for thousands of years. Over the course of several hundred years, the plant made its way through Texas, into Oklahoma, and then to the Ute. Just as they had with many other things introduced to them, the Navajo took the peyote religion and made it their own. Through the use of peyote in all-night prayer meetings, Hózhó, the quest for beauty, harmony, and balance, was again possible to achieve.

When the tribal council deliberated to ban peyote, only one councilman, Hola Tso, spoke in favor of its use. Tso cast the sole dissenting vote as the proposal to outlaw the use of peyote on the reservation passed. Collier supported the peyotists because he believed in the freedom of religion. However, he also acknowledged that the Navajo council should act in the best interest of the people. Therefore, although Collier disagreed with the council's action, he had to allow it to ban peyote. However, he refused to allow the use of federal funds to enforce the ban. Under tribal law, from the 1940s into the late 1950s, peyotists were harassed and jailed for the practice of their religion. Tribal police broke up prayer meetings, confiscated paraphernalia, and jailed the participants. Peyotists resorted to holding their meetings in remote areas to escape the attention of the police.

The members of the new religion challenged tribal law and sought to repeal the ban. They pointed out that their religion was important in addressing the emotional and mental distress caused by the loss of livestock. They also pointed out that the peyote religion required members to refrain from the use of alcohol, which was important because alcoholism was a problem on the reservation. In 1951, the Bureau of Indian Affairs estimated that 12 to 14 percent of the Navajo participated in peyote ceremonies. By 1965, 35 to 40 percent of the Navajo took part in peyote ceremonies. Seven years later, 40 to 50 percent of the population were peyotists.

Although many attempts were made to repeal the ban on peyote, it was not until Raymond Nakai became chairman of the Navajo tribe that it became possible to repeal the legislation. In

1967, the ban on the use of peyote was lifted when the Navajo Tribal Council passed a resolution that recognized peyotism. Today most Navajo have memberships in the Native American Church of Navajoland, while others are members of the Native American Church of the Four Corners or the Northern Navajoland Native American Church Association. Overall, the Navajo have one of the largest followings of this religion, with more than 60,000 members.

THE MOVE TO A WAGE ECONOMY

By 1945, federal Indian policy had transformed Navajo society. Livestock reduction had failed to address the problems of recovering the land. The efforts to garner more land had also not materialized. With their herds decimated, the Navajo looked to outside sources to sustain themselves. Wage labor replaced sheep and goats for subsistence. The Navajo's introduction to the wage economy had been through the New Deal conservation jobs that had come to the reservation. Those jobs were short-lived, though, and the Navajo had to look elsewhere to support themselves. In 1936, 54 percent of the Navajo had relied on livestock and agriculture for their livelihood; 34 percent relied on income from wages, and 6 percent relied on arts and crafts. By 1958, livestock and agriculture constituted only 10 percent of the source of Navajo livelihood while wages were 68 percent, and welfare, benefits, and railroad retirement represented 16 percent of income.

From the 1940s into the 1950s, federal officials reinstituted a policy of assimilation in which Navajo were encouraged to relocate to urban areas for employment and education opportunities. Relocation offices opened in border towns like Gallup, New Mexico, and Flagstaff, Arizona, to facilitate the entrance of Navajos into the American labor force. Relocation officers worked with employers in urban areas to introduce them to the culturally specific ways the Navajo workers might behave. The relocation workers also educated the Navajo about American work habits and cultural practices. For example, in 1948, the Bureau of Indian

Navajo code talkers serving with the U.S. Marines operate a radio near the front lines during World War II. The Navajo code was never broken and played a crucial role in the U.S. winning the war in the Pacific.

Affairs established the Navajo Placement Service to place work-ers in agricultural and railroad work. Prospective employers were encouraged to make Navajo workers feel as though they were part of their new community and were educated on Navajo cultural ways. They were told that the Navajo might miss work because they were expected to participate in ceremonies at home. One federal official declared that a problem for the Navajo was their strong ties to the reservation. As cited in *Working the Navajo Way*, the official said, "The Navajo is in general a primitive sort of indi-vidual. The wide world is a foreign world to him. He doesn't feel any happier than we would feel in the Navajo world."

WORLD WAR II
With the onset of World War II, attention from livestock reduction was diverted. In 1924, like other Native peoples, the Navajo were declared U.S. citizens, although they were not citizens of states like Arizona and New Mexico. In a display of patriotism, the Navajo Tribal Council passed a resolution supporting the United States in World War II. Recruiters came to Navajoland, and Navajos enlisted in the American military. At the beginning of the war, about 1,400 Navajo joined the armed forces. The Navajo called Adolf Hitler "mustache smeller" and Benito Mussolini "gourd chin." Overall, about 3,600 Navajo served in World War II. Federal officials approved of Navajo enlistments in the military for they appeared to provide a way to relieve population pressure on the reservation. Thousands of Navajo men and women left to enlist in the military and to work in defense-related industries. They also moved to cities to take advantage of wartime jobs.

REPORTS ON THE NAVAJO
In 1947, Charles G. Ross, secretary to the president of the United States, released a report on the condition of the Navajo. The report noted the impoverishment of the Navajo, the poor grazing lands, the small area of irrigated lands, and the need to develop a long-range plan to forestall a serious collapse of community life. The

report also recommended that the Navajo be encouraged to leave the reservation permanently—thus beginning the implementation of Termination policy, which intended to move Native peoples into the American mainstream through relocation programs. Secretary of the Interior Julius Krug announced that the need for off-reservation settlement of Navajo was urgent as the reservation could "support only 35,000 of the total Navajo population of 61,000." The Colorado River Indian Reservation, where Navajo and Hopi were being resettled and encouraged to farm, was proving a success.

On October 21, 1947, Assistant Secretary William E. Warne released a statement that was to be submitted to the House Appropriations Committee's Subcommittee on the Interior Department. The statement acknowledged that the Navajo had not enjoyed the same standard of living as other Americans. They were in need of quality health, education, welfare, and agricultural assistance. They also needed access to credit, soil conservation services, and road construction.

On June 27, 1949, a "Summary of Navajo Developments" was released. This report was a result of visits by three congressional subcommittees to the Navajo reservation in 1947. The report, "The Navajo," was submitted to Congress and recommended an appropriation of $90 million to be used over a period of 10 years to make capital improvements on the reservation. Congress did not pass any legislation for a long-range Navajo program. Finally, in 1950, in response to conditions on the Navajo and Hopi reservations, Congress passed the Navajo-Hopi Long Range Rehabilitation Act, which appropriated $88 million for infrastructure development on both reservations. In 1958, Congress added another $20 million for road construction. Federal officials hoped that the funds to create an infrastructure on Navajo lands would bolster the economy and, at the same time, connect the Navajo to the outside market. Paved roads, electricity, and telephones would go far to attract large-scale industries. The discovery of valuable natural resources also served as an incentive to develop Navajo lands.

(continues on page 112)

The Code Talkers

When Japan bombed Pearl Harbor on December 7, 1941, the Navajo, like many other Americans, were quick to join the fight to defend their country. More than 3,600 Navajo enlisted in the U.S. armed forces when President Franklin D. Roosevelt declared war on Japan and its allies. Twelve Navajo women also enlisted in the Army Air Corps. The Japanese army seemed invincible as it claimed territories in the Philippines, Southeast Asia, and Indonesia. The Japanese were also adept at breaking secret codes, much to the dismay of the United States.

Philip Johnston, a civil engineer and the son of missionaries who had lived on the Navajo reservation, learned about the need to develop a code that the Japanese could not decipher. Knowing that few outside of Arizona and New Mexico had information about the Navajo language and its intricacies, Johnston approached the marines at Camp Elliott, California, to share his plan to develop a code using the Navajo language. Although the marines were skeptical, they allowed Johnston and a few Navajo to demonstrate how the code would work. Impressed with the ability of the Navajo to relay messages in their language and then translate them into English, the marine recruiters went to Navajoland to enlist the first code talkers for service.

The first 29 Navajo recruits were sent to Camp Elliott in April 1942. They joined the 382nd Platoon, 4th Marine Division. After successfully completing boot camp, they were trained in communications. The men studied Morse code, semaphore signals, techniques of military message writing, wire laying, pole climbing, and other communication procedures. The soldiers used Navajo words for military terms, foreign countries, and other topics. A bomber plane now was *jeeshóó'* (buzzard), a submarine became *beeshlóó'* (iron fish), and a battleship became *łóótsoh* (whale). Each letter of the English alphabet underwent a transformation. In the code, *wólachíí'* (ant) stood for "a." *Shash* (bear) stood for "b." And *mosí* (cat) stood for "c."

After eight weeks of basic training, the Navajo men were sent overseas, where they played an important role in reclaiming territories that Japan held. Joining the initial 29 recruits were more than 400 Navajo men. They played key roles at Guadalcanal, Tarawa, Peleliu, and Iwo Jima. During the first 48 hours at Iwo Jima, the code talkers sent 800 messages without error. One major commented, "Without the Code Talkers, the Marines would never have taken Iwo Jima."

After World War II ended, the United States kept the code secret, and the code talkers returned to civilian life with virtually no recognition for their part in winning the war against the Japanese. At home, they continued to experience discrimination and racism. Indeed, the Navajo were not allowed to vote in New Mexico and Arizona until 1948.

Finally, after decades of silence, the code talkers were recognized for their patriotism. In 1968, the Defense Department declassified the Navajo code. At the 4th Marine Division's reunion in 1969, the marines made the code talkers their honored guests. In 1976, a television station in Phoenix, Arizona, helped to raise money to send the code talkers to Washington, D.C, where they proudly marched in the nation's bicentennial parade. In 1982, the U.S. Senate passed a resolution and President Ronald Reagan declared August 14 as "National Navajo Code Talkers Day." A Code Talkers Association was formed, and members represented the Navajo Nation in ceremonies and parades throughout the country.

On July 26, 2001, four of the surviving code talkers from the original 29 and families representing the other 25, traveled to Washington, D.C., to receive the Congressional Gold Medal, the highest civilian award Congress can bestow. John Brown Jr., Chester Nez, Lloyd Oliver, and Allen Dale June traveled with their families to receive recognition for their loyalty to the United States.

(continues)

(continued)

President George W. Bush said, "Today, we honor 29 Native Americans who, in a desperate hour, gave their country a service only they could give. Today we give these exceptional Marines the recognition they earned so long ago." In a separate ceremony, the other code talkers were awarded the Silver Congressional Medal. In September 2010, Allen Dale June, one of the original 29 code talkers, died at the age of 91. During his service to the United States, June attained the rank of sergeant. Too young to enlist in the Marines, he was turned away at the recruiting station in his hometown of Kaibeto on the Navajo Nation. He traveled to the nearby community of Chinle, where he lied about his age and forged his father's signature in order to enlist. In February 2011, another member of the elite code talkers, Johnny Dale Alfred, died at the age of 91. Alfred joined the marines when he was 22 years old and was among the 439 Navajo men who joined the code talkers. In paying tribute to the code talkers, America honored the Navajo men's courage, intelligence and perseverance, and their defense of their country.

(continued from page 109)

THE ROOTS OF THE MODERN NAVAJO NATION

John Collier's efforts to reform tribal governments so that Native leaders would have more authority and influence also shaped Navajo tribal governance. Although the 1934 Indian Reorganization Act (IRA) signaled a new era in Indian country, one of self-determination, for the Navajo, the timing was wrong. The IRA gave Indian communities the right to develop constitutions, form representative tribal councils, and access certain federal loans. When Collier brought his ideas about government reform to Navajo leaders, they were suspicious because at the same time, they were expected to comply with Collier's livestock reduction policies. Jacob Morgan led the opposition to the act, and Chee Dodge, a revered tribal leader, was hesitant in his support. In June 1935, the Navajo cast their vote. Linking the IRA to livestock reduction, the Navajo people narrowly rejected the act, 8,197 to 7,679. Collier had anticipated the measure passing and was deeply disappointed at the response. He thought that adopting a constitution would give the Navajo considerable power in dealing with tribal affairs that had been handled by the U.S. secretary of the interior. Although the Navajo rejected the IRA, which was intended to reformulate tribal governments on the American democratic model, they did come under a government similar to that outlined by the IRA.

Navajo governance had begun a transition in the 1860s, when the Navajo came under American rule. The United States had worked to divest traditional leaders of their political influence beginning in the early reservation period. Leaders were expected to carry out the Indian agent's wishes. Leaders like Manuelito, Barboncito, and Ganado Mucho had survived the war on their people and retained a measure of influence into the late nineteenth century. With the appointment of Chee Dodge as a leader, a new era in Navajo leadership took form. Chee Dodge was probably born in the 1850s to a Navajo woman and a non-Navajo man, whom some thought might have been the Indian agent Henry Dodge or a Hispanic man. Because of his mixed parentage and the death of his mother before the Long Walk, Dodge was paid special attention by Indian agents. He learned to speak English fluently and acquired a Western business sense. By 1882, he was the interpreter at Fort Defiance and then became a successful stockman and businessman. His son, Thomas Dodge, became chairman of the Navajo Tribe after his father stepped down.

With the discovery of oil and gas in the northern region of the Navajo reservation, federal officials needed an efficient way to garner Navajo support for the development of their natural resources. In 1922, the first tribal council was convened for the purpose of rubber-stamping the approval of leases with mining companies. The actions of the tribal council during Collier's administration,

The Later Life of Manuelito

Upon his return to Dinétah, Manuelito remained an influential leader among his people. He was appointed head of the first Navajo police on the reservation. In 1874, he traveled with his wife and other Navajo leaders to Washington, D.C., to meet President Ulysses S. Grant. In the 1880s, he sent two of his sons to Carlisle Indian Industrial School in Carlisle, Pennsylvania, as a message to his people that they should not fear Western education for their children. The children would return home and use their acquired knowledge for the betterment of their people.

In 1894, Manuelito died from a combination of diseases, including alcoholism. His widow, Juanita, whose Navajo name was Asdzáá Tł'ógi (Lady Weaver), and his daughters carried on his messages about the importance of education for the children and the retention of land for the coming generations. Today, Manuelito remains a popular hero image for the Navajo, who have composed songs and poetry about him. His people remember his struggle to keep Navajo lands, his commitment to Navajo sovereignty, and his avocation of an American education for Navajo children so that they might protect their people. Born during a time of great strife for his people, Manuelito knew personally the kind of force and violence that foreigners were capable of using against indigenous peoples.

when the members hesitantly endorsed Collier's program for livestock reduction, indicate how little authority or power the council had. The effort to reform the Navajo government and to establish a constitution was seen as another coercive act by the Indian commissioner, and therefore rejected.

In 1968, under Chairman Raymond Nakai, the Navajo Tribe changed its name to the Navajo Nation. The change was a response to the atmosphere of the Red Power era and part of the call to reclaim the sovereignty of tribal nations. From governance based upon the leadership of leaders like Barboncito and Manuelito, who gained their authority by the blessings of the people, the people saw their leaders subordinated to U.S. authority, which was intended to render them dependent on the largesse of the federal government. Nakai's proclamation of a sovereign Navajo nation was a call to remember the ancestors' struggles and determination to uphold Navajo sovereignty. Today, the struggle continues as the Navajo and their leaders discuss and debate what it means to be a sovereign Navajo Nation.

The early twentieth century was a time of many transitions for the Navajo Tribe and its people. Their experiences under American rule in the nineteenth century, after a majority of their people had returned from the Bosque Redondo reservation to their homeland, were defined by a return to patterns of livestock raising and agriculture. To some extent, the People had successfully transitioned from the hated Hwéeldi, the Bosque Redondo reservation, to their homeland and once again prospered. Due to a number of reasons, however, including contests over land with non-Indian settlers and ranchers, the push to force them to remain on a small reservation base, and the environmental crisis, the Navajo were faced with new challenges when Indian commissioner John Collier carried out livestock reduction. These changes took place in several ways, including practices of land use, education, religion, the economy, and government structure, and have had far-reaching effects on the Navajo. Today, they are still working to resolve many of the issues and problems rooted in livestock reduction.

The Promises and Challenges of the Twentieth and Twenty-first Centuries

In 1952, the Navajo Tribe officially adopted John Claw Jr.'s design for a tribal seal. The seal depicted the sacred geography of Navajoland: Within the four sacred mountains, a sheep, a cow, and a horse symbolize the Navajo livestock industry. At the top of the seal, the sun provides its power to the land and people. At the bottom of the image, cornstalks symbolize their significance as sustainers of life. In 1988, the Navajo Nation Council amended the words "Great Seal of the Navajo Tribe" on the seal to "Great Seal of the Navajo Nation." The change from the term "tribe" to "nation" signified a turn nationally, during the era of Red Power, in how Native peoples saw themselves, particularly in relationship to the United States. For the Navajo, the period from the 1960s into the 1980s was a time to assert their sovereignty as a nation and insist that the United States shoulder its responsibility to behave in a moral and just way toward them.

This chapter explores developments in the last half of the twentieth century up to the present by exploring how the national mood in Indian country called for justice at a time when people of color and women were demanding their civil rights. In contrast, the Navajo, like other Native peoples, raised awareness of their unique status as citizens of their respective tribal nations and began a revival movement to reclaim traditional values based upon the philosophy of Hózhó—balance, beauty, and harmony. In what ways did the Navajo Nation exercise its sovereignty? How did tribal and community leaders respond to the challenges wrought by the creation of their dependency upon the United States? In what ways do the values and teachings founded in the philosophy of Hózhó continue to manifest in Navajo communities?

In the early twentieth century, American photographer Laura Gilpin visited Navajo country when a friend received a job offer as a field nurse. Enthralled with the land and the people, she captured her impressions on film and published them as *The Enduring Navaho,* which offers glimpses of conditions on the reservation from the 1930s to the 1950s. Navajo women pose in elaborate velvet blouses and skirts and are adorned with turquoise and silver jewelry. In some photographs, images of "tradition" are juxtaposed with the "modern" to signify changes that the Navajo had undergone. Gilpin intended to relay the message that the Navajo had not vanished but that the "enduring" people had met change with resilience. Gilpin professed faith in the ability of the Navajo people to adapt to new ways.

In contrast to Gilpin's romantic depictions of the Navajo, federal reports in the 1950s indicated that a majority of them lived in poverty, the land remained in poor condition, and little of the land had access to water sources. The Navajo were not living the American dream. The Navajo-Hopi Long Range Rehabilitation Act, passed in 1950, intended to build infrastructure in Navajo country. By the 1960s, roads had been paved and businesses in urban communities were appearing, and in the 1970s, local schools were finally built. In the 1950s and 1960s, under the auspices of federal officials, tribal leaders negotiated leases for gas, coal, and uranium, and the creation of infrastructure allowed access to natural resources for development. These early leases signed by Navajo leaders were exploitative. By the 1970s and 1980s, however, Navajo leaders tested their nation's sovereign rights and demanded that energy companies pay taxes. Challenging energy companies was but one way that Navajo leaders sought to alleviate chronic poverty and all the social ills that accompanied it.

The 2000 census showed the Navajo population at 275,000. Of the 180,000 people who live within the boundaries of the Navajo Nation, 175,000 are Navajo. More than 100,000 Navajo live in urban areas like Phoenix and Flagstaff, Arizona; Albuquerque, Gallup, and Farmington, New Mexico; and Barstow and Los Angeles, California. The census also shows that the Navajo population is young, with the median age between 18 and 24. Interestingly, of the Native Americans who filled out the census forms, more than 90 percent of Navajo identified themselves as Navajo only. In contrast, other Native Americans noted that they were of mixed heritage. Further, the census gave an indication that the Navajo, like the rest of Americans, were urbanized. On the Navajo Nation, urban communities have grown around administrative centers such as Window Rock, Fort Defiance, Tuba City, Shiprock, and Kayenta.

A TIME TO REFLECT

The year 1968 is a benchmark for the Navajo people, for it was 100 years earlier that the Treaty of 1868 was signed and the Navajo were allowed to return to their beloved homeland. Under the leadership of Chairman Raymond Nakai, the Navajo marked the 100th anniversary of the return from Hwéeldi with cultural events that included essay contests, publications on Navajo history by non-Indian scholars, and articles on Navajo history printed in the *Navajo Times*. Major events included a reenactment of the Long

Walk and the signing of the treaty, which involved Navajos returning to Hwéeldi. The annual Navajo fair highlighted the centennial with its theme, "A Century of Progress." What was the state
of the Navajo tribe 100 years after the People had endured one of
the most traumatic experiences of their collectivity? In 100 years,
had they been very much changed by their exposure to American
assimilation policies? How had they fared under American rule?

Nakai's speech, delivered at the opening of the centennial year,
recapped what the return from the Bosque Redondo meant for
the Navajo: "The Century of Progress which we commemorate has
not been an easy 100 years. It was initiated by the tragic and heart-
breaking 'long march' from Fort Sumner. It marked a struggle
of a proud people, accustomed to roam unfettered over the vast
expanses of this great western United States." Nakai went on to say,
"All in all, this past 100 years does reflect great progress on the part
of our people." Significantly, the definition of "progress" for tribal
leaders has meant the development of resources in ways intended
to raise the living standards of the Navajo people; however, "progress" also meant grappling with a sense of loss of culturally relevant teachings and practices, which was also a theme during the
centennial.

The discovery of oil and gas in the 1920s in the Aneth, Utah,
and Shiprock, New Mexico, regions led to more discoveries of
natural resources, including coal and uranium, in the decades
before the centennial. The San Juan region holds petroleum, natural gas, and vast deposits of coal. Large leases were granted to Utah
International and El Paso Natural Gas Company-Consolidated
Coal Company. Near Gallup, New Mexico, the Pittsburg and
Midway Coal Company operated coalfields. The Peabody Coal
Company mines a third major region of coal deposits. The mining
of these resources has been the major source of revenues for the
Navajo Tribe. The money that went into the tribal treasury slowly
increased as tribal leaders signed leases with these companies. By
1962, the Navajo Tribe netted $15,139,135 for oil and uranium.

The royalties from coal totaled $24,320 each year in 1960, 1961, and 1962. The coal leases, however, were way below market value, and in the next decade the federal government was highly criticized for dictating how tribes like the Navajo were to act in signing leases with mining companies.

In the 1970s and 1980s, tribal leaders like Peter MacDonald and Peterson Zah, both of whom had college degrees, challenged the way business had been done with mining companies. For one, until the 1970s, the Navajo Nation did not collect taxes to finance operations, although it was entitled to do so. Amazingly, while the Navajo Nation was not collecting taxes on non-Indian businesses operating on its land, the states of Arizona, New Mexico, and Utah were taxing these businesses. In fact, these governments were receiving more income for the development of Navajo Nation resources than the Nation was earning. For example, in 1972, the Navajo Nation received $1.4 million in royalties for the coal from the Four Corners Power Plant while the state, county, and local governments received $7.2 million. As a result, the Navajo Nation under the MacDonald administration established a Navajo Tax Commission, which set up two ordinances to correct tax equities. Of course, the businesses immediately objected, for Indian tribes were not supposed to expect to exercise their sovereignty. In another example of the Navajo Nation realizing its sovereign powers, Kerr-McGee Corporation sued the Navajo Nation when the company was served notice that it would have to pay taxes. In 1985, the U.S. Supreme Court, in *Kerr-McGee Corporation v. the Navajo Tribe*, acknowledged that the tribe had the sovereign power to enact and impose tax laws with approval of the Interior Department.

From the 1960s to the 1980s, tribal leaders, inspired by the critical consciousness-raising of the times, exercised national sovereignty and tried to improve conditions for their people. The problems and issues they faced were many. However, the dependence on revenues from the development of natural resources raised objections from a segment of the Navajo population that continue to the present. Some of the most vocal resisters have been women from Big Mountain in northern Arizona, for they charge that the major reason for the relocation of Navajo and Hopi from lands awarded to the other tribe in the 1974 Navajo-Hopi Land Settlement Act centers on the natural resources in the region, including coal and water.

In 1996, after more than two decades of Navajo resistance to removal, Congress enacted Public Law 104-301, the Navajo-Hopi Land Dispute Settlement Act, which implemented the Accommodation Agreement. The act ratified the settlement of four claims of the Hopi nation against the federal government and authorized the Hopi to exercise jurisdiction over the land awarded to them earlier. The Accommodation Agreement provided an avenue for Navajo families to remain in their homes. Each Accommodation Agreement allows for 3 acres (1.2 ha) plus 10 acres (4 ha) of farmland. Grazing rights depended upon a permit from the Hopi Tribe. The leases are not transferable and are only good for the duration of the original signer's life, although in some cases the Hopi will consider renewing a lease for another 75 years. Five hundred and seventy Navajos signed the agreement that allowed them to stay on Hopi partitioned lands for 75 years. The agreement also called for the U.S. government and the Navajo Nation to pay the Hopi more than $50 million as part of the settlement.

Today a handful of Navajo still live at Big Mountain, on Hopi partition land, and refuse to sign the Accommodation Agreement. On March 31, 1997, yet another deadline for the complete removal of Navajo from Hopi partition land passed. In the summer of 2001, in an effort to force Navajo out of the area, Hopi officials destroyed a Sun Dance ceremonial ground at Big Mountain, saying that the Navajo were using the ceremony as a political tool and that they were illegally squatting on Hopi land.

In 1978, Thayer Scudder, an expert on the relocation of rural populations, testified before Congress that the Navajo would suffer great hardships if they were forced to leave the only homes they had ever known. Today, stories of great stress, including psychological and emotional distress, of the debilitating consequences of forced relocation, circulate among the Navajo people. Newlands, one area where the Navajo were relocated, near Sanders, Arizona, was recognized in 1992 as a new chapter, Nahata Dziil. This new chapter was built according to urban plans, in which homes are close to each other and livestock is not allowed, a hardship for Navajo who depend upon livestock for their livelihood.

The relocation controversy has followed the mining of the Black Mesa, which many area residents have criticized. Peabody Coal Company opened its strip mines in 1970 and has relied on Navajo and Hopi water to move 5 million tons (4.5 million metric tons) of coal annually to the Mohave Generating Station near Laughlin, Nevada. From the Kayenta strip mine, which is not far from the Black Mesa mine, Peabody moves 7 million tons of coal (6.3 million metric tons) annually by conveyor belt 17 miles (27 km) to storage silos near Black Mesa. From there, the coal is shipped 80 miles (129 km) to the Navajo Generating Station near Page, Arizona. Over the years Navajo residents have complained about the effect of the mines on their quality of life. In addition to being forced to move to make way for mines, they observe that little effort has been made to reclaim mined land and that the air and water are polluted. The Navajo remain troubled by the ongoing exploitation of their land, but they are also equally concerned about the jobs that will be lost if the mines close. The mines have pumped billions of dollars into the Navajo and Hopi economies through employee salaries, lease payments, mining royalties, tribal taxes, charitable donations, and scholarships.

Growing concern among local Navajo and Hopi residents has united them in the fight to stop Peabody's continued use of pristine underground water. Grassroots organizations like Black

Waldine Yazzie, a Navajo woman scheduled to be relocated, holds a sign that reads, "Go Ahead, Make My Day." Yazzie was participating in a 1986 protest march in Big Mountain, Arizona.

Mesa Trust, Black Mesa Water Coalition, To'Nizhoni Ani, and the Natural Resources Defense Council have emerged to oppose Peabody's use of water drawn from the underground aquifer known as the Navajo or N-aquifer. Over the last 10 years, continued opposition is forcing U.S. officials to scrutinize the Peabody mining operations. In 2005, the Mohave Generating Station shut down as a result of a Clean Air Act lawsuit, and consequently the mine at Black Mesa was forced to close. For the Navajo and Hopi opposed to the way Peabody Coal has done business with both tribes, the lawsuit was a small victory in the ongoing struggle to stop the exploitation of tribal land, natural resources, and water. In 2010, Peabody Coal tried to reopen its Black Mesa mine, but strong opposition from Navajo environmental activists and their allies have kept it closed. The second mine on Black Mesa at Kayenta remains open and supplies the Navajo Generating Station, which has provided power to Las Vegas, Los Angeles, Phoenix, and other urban areas for three decades.

URANIUM MINING

Uranium was another resource that was mined on the Navajo lands. In the 1940s and 1950s, the Bureau of Indian Affairs encouraged Navajo leaders to accept leases with corporations to open Navajo land to uranium mining. Initially seen as a boost to the economy, hundreds of Navajo men worked in these mines. In a reservation economy with so few jobs, mining uranium assured the men that they could stay home and support their families. From 1952 to 1963, Kerr-McGee operated mines near Shiprock.

In 1996 Timothy Benally, a former uranium miner, was named the director of the Navajo Uranium Workers Program, established in 1990 to identify former Navajo miners and to assist them in dealing with the Radiation Exposure Compensation Act (RECA). RECA was to pay compassionate compensation to uranium miners who worked during the Cold War era of 1947 to 1971. The program proved to be useful as Navajo miners found that, because of their traditional practices and their limited access to quality medical care, they did not fit the criteria established for compensation. The miners and their families continue to wrestle with the consequences of uranium mining, including the need to change the criteria for RECA so that more retired Navajo miners qualify for compensation.

On April 25, 2005, Tribal President Joe Shirley Jr. signed into law the Diné Natural Resources Protection Act, which banned conventional uranium mining in the Navajo Nation and placed a long-term moratorium on uranium processing. It is believed to be the first Native American tribal law banning uranium mining. Key to the passage of the act were Navajo citizens who educated their communities and tribal council members about the threats to their land and health if Hydro Resources Inc. received approval to mine four areas near Crownpoint and Church Rock, New Mexico. To date, Hydro Resources has not been deterred by the Navajo Nation's injunction, but seeks to mine uranium along the nation's borders. In March 2010, the U.S. Court of Appeals for the Tenth Circuit rejected a lawsuit brought by Eastern Navajo Diné Against Uranium Mining (ENDAUM) and the Southwest Research and Information Center to stop Hydro Resources from mining just outside the Navajo Nation's borders. ENDAUM and the Southwest Research and Information Center charged that the mining would contaminate the drinking water of 15,000 people living in the Crownpoint and Church Rock communities.

In 2011, Navajo at the community level remain adamant about the dangers of uranium mining. When newly-elected president Ben Shelly and vice president Rex Lee Jim accepted $10,000 from URI, a Texas-based company that plans to begin uranium mining operations in the eastern region of Navajoland, to defray costs for their inauguration, Navajo citizens protested. Said Norman Brown of the grassroots group Diné Bidziil, "URI is spending millions of dollars fighting the Navajo Nation's ban on uranium. . . . We find that accepting contributions from URI lacks integrity and is disrespectful of the suffering of the people for the last 40 to 50 years."

The Return of Navajo Boy, a film codirected by Jeffrey Spitz and Bennie Klain, depicts the effects of uranium mining on the land and on Navajo families. The documentary follows a Navajo family in Monument Valley that was affected for generations by uranium mining. One family member, Elsie Mae Begay, tells how her mother died of cancer, which is associated with exposure to radiation from mining activities. Men came home from the mines with the radioactive dirt on their clothes. At the mines, the workers drank from nearby springs and brought home radioactive building materials, which they used to make homes. Begay's father worked in the uranium mines, as did Begay's husband. Today, many of her kin have died from cancer. Begay is but one of thousands of families affected by the mining, and even in 2011, the

Protestors including Dalenna Long (*above*) speak out against uranium mining near Navajo communities in New Mexico.

U.S. Environmental Protection Agency (EPA) has yet to clean up high-level radiation areas. The Navajo realize that they have paid high prices for allowing uranium mining on their land.

CULTURAL REVITALIZATION

From the 1960s into the 1970s, tribal leaders exerted the sovereign powers of the Navajo Nation in ways intended to address the state of the land and people. Leaders continued to prioritize the education of their young people by looking for models that centered on Navajo teachings and funding scholarships for students going to colleges and universities. In the 1990s, more Bureau of Indian Affairs schools came under local control. While local control is viewed as a positive step toward reclaiming Navajo education, a web of schools is still overseen by various federal, state, and tribal administrations. In 2004, President Joe Shirley Jr. signed the Navajo in Education Sovereignty Act, which established the Navajo Board of Education and the Navajo Nation Department of Diné Education. The act is a response to New Mexico and Arizona reports that Navajo students, like many of their non-Indian counterparts throughout the area, are failing national standards that all students should meet to graduate from high school. The creation of these entities has yet to unify the curriculums taught in all schools on Navajoland and set education standards that match those of New Mexico and Arizona.

The cultural revitalization of the 1960s and 1970s included the imperative to reclaim the authority to tell the Navajo side of stories. Navajo writers Luci Tapahonso, Laura Tohe, Esther Belin, Irwin Bitsui, and Irvin Morris use contemporary forms of narratives and poetry to convey traditional knowledge to a receptive Navajo audience, many of whom belong to a growing younger population. These creative artists offer portrayals of contemporary Navajo life with all of its trials and tribulations. Grandmothers and grandfathers, children and babies, rodeo cowboys, and boarding schools appear in stories that paint colorful Navajo lives. Questions about the consequences of history, identity and cultural loss, and the value of cultural teachings are only a few of the topics these writers and poets touch upon. Their works do not flinch from a history of colonialism.

While formal education has yet to see a truly Navajo-centered curriculum, individual Navajo have shouldered the responsibility to use their education, talents, and skills to promote and preserve traditional values through contemporary forms shaped by exposure to modern American society. For example, performance artists Marilyn Help and Radmilla Cody are always busy with daily life—Help is a Navajo culture and language teacher at an elementary school and Cody is a student at Northern Arizona University.

When they are not at school, they are providing culturally relevant lessons in Navajo communities. To enhance an appreciation for Navajo values, Help coauthored a book with University of New Mexico professor Ellen McCullough-Brabson, *We'll Be in Your Mountains, We'll Be in Your Songs: A Navajo Woman Sings.* As a young woman, Help won the Miss Navajo title, among several other pageant titles. After representing the Navajo people as Miss Navajo, Help went on to raise her family and attain a bachelor's degree in elementary education. Like so many Navajo, she finds that a return to tradition is a way to ensure the continuity of the People. Indeed, her fluency in Navajo and American ways, including the ability to speak Navajo and English easily, is evidence of the strength of the old ways as more and more Navajo seek to integrate traditional ways into their lives.

Radmilla Cody is also a former Miss Navajo who shares through music her life story of being racially mixed—her mother is Navajo and her father is African American. In the years after her reign, Cody served jail time for her involvement in her boyfriend's drug operations. In her message to the Navajo people about her relationship with her boyfriend, Cody explained that she was involved in a web of violence and feared for her life if she did not remain silent about her boyfriend's activities. Cody's messages to young Navajo about racism, prejudices against racially mixed Navajo, and domestic violence are featured in a documentary of her experiences, titled *Hearing Radmilla.*

Other areas of cultural revitalization are taking place in music and film. For example, the Navajo punk rock band Blackfire is composed of the Benally siblings: two brothers, Clayson and Klee, and their sister, Jeneda. As children they were introduced to traditional Navajo music by their father, Jones, who is also a traditional healer. Originally from Black Mesa, in the heart of the land under dispute with the Hopi, the Benally siblings learned early about the history of their people and the resistance of the Navajo who refuse to be relocated. Blackfire uses its music to advocate for Native peoples and the Navajo. The band's traditional Native American, punk rock, and "Alter-Native" style conveys sociopolitical messages regarding government oppression, relocation of indigenous people, eco-cide, genocide, domestic violence, and human rights.

Navajo like Bennie Klain also advocate for justice through the medium of film. In 2008, Klain completed *Weaving Worlds*, which presents a compelling and intimate portrait of economic and cultural survival through the art of weaving in the face of increased globalization. Klain interviewed a host of people, from weavers to traders, who are part of the Navajo weaving world. As Klain shows, Navajo artists struggle to maintain pride and cultural vitality through creating their textiles and "reweaving the world." Klain collaborated with Navajos and others like anthropologist Kathy M'Closkey, who shows through her study how weavers lost control of the production of their textiles. By the end of the nineteenth century, the textiles that Navajo women spent so many laborious hours weaving were no longer made for Navajo use but were popularized as rugs and wall hangings for collectors and tourists who began to flood into the Southwest. Navajo women, for the most part, have lost control of the sales of their textiles. Today, weavers see very little return for their labor. Nevertheless, weaving as a traditional art form has survived to the present. The art of weaving is a significant manifestation of tradition that was given to them by Grandmother Spider.

Today, Navajo women continue to weave, and more recently, men have come into the public eye as skilled weavers in their own right. While the market for Navajo-made textiles might ebb and flow, weavers continue to turn out spectacular textiles that rival those made by their grandmothers. In attempts to take control of the textile market, in some areas of Navajoland, weavers have created cooperatives and established auctions like the one that takes place in Crownpoint, New Mexico. Bonnie Benally Yazzie is the director of the Eastern Navajo Weavers Association. She spends many hours teaching weaving to anyone who is willing to learn.

Mothers and daughters take Yazzie's instructions as a way to return to cultural values, and at the same time, they use the lessons to renew their mother-daughter bonds. At auction time, she educates buyers about the textiles and about the threat that weavers face as knockoffs from Mexico and overseas flood the market, making it difficult for weavers to get fair value for their handmade products.

Today's Navajo, like their grandmothers and grandfathers once did, also embrace certain American cultural traditions and practices that are easily integrated into their way of life. In particular, American sports such as basketball, cross-country, golf, and rodeo are favorites in many Navajo communities. Perhaps because it is easy to put up a hoop outside a home, basketball is a popular sport that draws crowds at local high schools. Many high school teams compete successfully and go on to state championship games in Phoenix, Arizona, and Albuquerque, New Mexico. Undeterred by the hundreds of miles required to attend the games in cities, fans follow their favorite teams and fill the gyms to capacity. Few colleges recruit Navajo athletes and even fewer athletes make it to the professional circuit. But when they do, athletes like Ryneldi Becenti draw huge Navajo and Native American fans. Becenti played for the Arizona State University Sun Devils. In 1992, she was the leading scorer on a team that won 20 games. With Becenti on board, the team won a bid to play in the NCAA tournament for the first time in nine years. The basketball players could not help but comment on the Navajo fans who often filled the gym to capacity, since the women usually played in almost empty gyms before Becenti joined the team. Becenti went on to play for the U.S. team in the World University Games in 1993.

MODERN GOVERNMENT

Since Raymond Nakai's administration from 1963 to 1969, the Navajo government has seen changes intended to realize its sovereign status. For example, Dinébeiina Nahiilna Be Agaditahe (DNA), or "Attorneys who contribute to the economic revitalization of the people," was established to give the Navajo community access to legal services. In 1968, the passage of the Indian Civil Rights Act imposed most of the provisions of the U.S. Bill of Rights on tribal governments. The 1990s saw the implementation of amendments to the tribal code and government reform, mostly as a result of the power that Peter MacDonald had amassed during his administration. The 1989 struggle for power between pro- and anti-MacDonald supporters highlighted the consequences of not having a formal tribal constitution. As a result of the problems with MacDonald's administration, the Navajo Nation government took measures to reduce the president's power in December 1989, by passing a landmark resolution amending Title II of the Tribal Code. The reforms created the position of a Speaker of the House, who presides over the Navajo Nation Council. The reforms also reduced the number of standing committees and gave the speaker the power to appoint members to legislative committees, removing it from the president.

In further movements toward government reform, when Albert Hale was elected president in 1995, he called for a return of power to the Navajo people. The Navajo Nation Local Governance Act in 1998 gave chapters a chance to participate in decisions of local importance. Early in his presidency, however, Hale was charged with ethical violations, including spending tribal money inappropriately, accepting bribes, and having an extramarital affair. Amid these allegations, Hale stepped down. The government reforms that reduced the president's power seemed to be working as Hale left office without the conflict that had ensued when the tribal council forced Peter MacDonald from office.

After Hale, several interim presidents served. Thomas Atcitty served only four months after being accused of accepting gifts from corporations. Milton Bluehouse then took over the presidency.

In 1998, 14 people declared their candidacy for president. LeNora Y. Fulton, a council delegate from Fort Defiance and the second woman to run for the highest office in Navajoland, was one of the contenders. The first woman, Kay Curley Bennett, ran in 1986 and 1990. Fulton's decision to run for president raised discussions among the Navajo about whether a woman should lead the largest Indian nation in the United States. Based upon a traditional story that warned about chaos in society if a woman ever held the highest leadership role, some Navajo felt that women should not become president. Fulton addressed the contention by arguing that traditional stories also convey the significance of both male and female roles for the People's survival. Although Fulton was not successful in her bid, her candidacy brought attention to women in leadership roles throughout Indian country.

In 2006 and 2010, Lynda Lovejoy attempted to break the barrier of men assuming the presidency. Just as the women before her had met with criticism, so too did Lovejoy, who was appointed a New Mexico senator when Leonard Tsosie resigned to take his seat on the Navajo Nation Council in January 2007. In her 2010 bid, many Navajo were surprised to see her survive the primary elections with a strong lead. However, Lovejoy's candidacy again brought to the surface questions about Navajo women's proper place in their society. National attention was also trained on Navajo politics as onlookers wondered if the Navajo Nation had not yet accorded women equal rights, while Navajo and other Natives pondered questions about the meaning and significance of "tradition." In interviews, Lovejoy declared that a woman as president would "clean house" and "bring a real motherly, nurturing approach" to the leadership. In both of her campaigns, Lovejoy was unsuccessful, and in 2011, former Navajo Nation vice president Ben Shelly became president.

Although the Navajo still might have vigorous debates and discussions on whether a woman can lead the Nation, they do acknowledge that in Navajo traditional society women were accorded a considerable amount of respect for their contributions to the well-being of their communities and families. Indeed, in these discussions, the name of one of the most prominent political figures, Annie Wauneka, is invoked. Wauneka was the daughter of the first chairman of the Navajo Tribe, Chee Dodge. She was schooled by her father on the nature of politics and was elected to the tribal council in 1951. She served for the next 30 years. Often the sole woman on the council, Wauneka served as a role model for women who aspired to public office. Her achievements included the eradication of diseases such as tuberculosis on the reservation, which led President John F. Kennedy to present the Presidential Medal of Freedom to her in 1963, the highest civil honor an individual can be awarded during peacetime.

As current president of the Navajo Nation, Ben Shelly inherits its financial woes. The closure of the mine at Black Mesa makes tribal leaders aware that they must find new sources of revenue. In the 1990s, in efforts to improve economic opportunities, Indian nations looked to gaming. While many tribes have created successful casinos and put the profits toward improving their communities, others have not fared as well. In 1994 and 1997, the Navajo Nation Council put gaming referendums before voters. Both times the Navajo rejected gaming. Many Navajo opposed gaming because traditional beliefs link gaming with excess and immorality. They also worried about the negative consequences of gaming, especially as the casinos would rely on Navajo clientele. Undeterred by the rejection, President Kelsey Begaye signed the first gaming ordinance in 2001.

The first casino, named Fire Rock, was established just east of Gallup, New Mexico, in 2008. Immensely popular with the Navajo, the casino's parking lot is almost always full, no matter the time of day. In 2009, the casino's chief operating officer expressed delight that the business was doing so well, although profits have been kept secret so far. Fire Rock's success led the Navajo Nation to open its second casino at Hogback, in upper Fruitland, New Mexico, in October 2010. Other casinos in Arizona are also in the planning stages. Many Navajo remain troubled about the consequences of gaming, especially because the main clientele of the two casinos has been Navajo.

A project that enhances local control for communities and shows promise for the Navajo Nation has been the establishment of Kayenta Township. On November 5, 1985, the Navajo Nation Council withdrew 3,606 acres (1,459 ha) of Navajo trust lands to create Kayenta Township. For decades citizens had been critical of the lack of development and civic management on Navajoland. Finally, after years of endless procedures and political wrangling, Kayenta Township was formally established when the council

Presidential Medal of Honor recipient Annie Wauneka (*left*) visits a Navajo family. The daughter of Chee Dodge, the Navajo Tribe's first chairman, Wauneka served on the tribal council for 30 years and made many important contributions.

passed a resolution to create the Kayenta Retail Sales Tax Project. The council authorized an election by voters living within the township boundaries to serve as commissioners. In the first eighteen months of its incorporation, the township's tax brought in $670,834. Residents began to see improvements, including the construction of a post office, a waste transfer station to take care of the dumping and trash problem, and the development of a 300-home subdivision. Even today, in other parts of Navajoland, similar improvements need to be made because problems, such as trash dumping in ravines, remain widespread. Adequate housing also remains a formidable obstacle for Navajo families. In 2010, the township was busy with three new developments: the Kayenta Alternative Health Care Facility, the Native American Technical Institute, and the Kayenta Public Safety Building. Kayenta Township remains a positive example of how local control can work.

WATER ISSUES

On December 29, 2004, after three years of review, the Navajo Nation Council passed a resolution to settle Navajo claims to the San Juan River. The attempts to settle Navajo water rights are not without opposition and controversy. In one of the first council deliberations on the issue, delegate Hope MacDonald-Lonetree from Tuba City reminded her fellow delegates that the Navajo Nation is a sovereign entity that should not give away its water rights simply to quiet non-Indians who contest Navajo rights. Her father, Peter MacDonald, also voiced his opposition in a commentary published in the *Navajo Times*. MacDonald, who was released from a federal prison in 1999 after serving seven years of a 14-year sentence for fraud, extortion, riot, bribery, and corruption, urged Navajo leaders and the community to retain water rights. As he noted, the Winters Doctrine of 1906 recognizes Navajo rights before other claimants to the water. Navajo citizens like Peter June Cordell wrote letters to the *Navajo Times* and argued that leaders should not settle for less than what the Nation was entitled to.

Finally, on December 22, 2005, after several hours of having the water rights settlement read into the record, the council voted to accept the resolution that would clarify Navajo water rights. The San Juan River Settlement recognizes the Navajo Nation's right to more than 606,060 acre-feet of diverted water annually (about 56 percent of the total available for use) and provides $800 million from the state of New Mexico to build the Navajo-Gallup Water Supply Project by December 2020—providing municipal water to chapters in the eastern and central areas of Navajoland. The settlement does not include funding to complete the canal system for the Navajo Indian Irrigation Project, which was supposed to be completed under a water rights settlement agreement made in the 1970s. Water would also be supplied for the Fruitland-Cambridge Irrigation Project, the Hogback-Cudei Irrigation Project, and several other smaller irrigation projects. Navajo activists also charged that a planned pipeline was intended to provide water to the proposed Desert Rock coal plant, a 1,500-megawatt facility to be built 25 miles (40 km) outside of Farmington, New Mexico, on the Navajo Nation. In more recent developments, the Navajo Nation settled another water rights case concerning the lower Colorado River. And once again, Navajos came to Window Rock to protest their leaders' actions.

FURTHER REFORMS

The new century brought additional government reform. In his second term as president of the Navajo Nation, Joe Shirley Jr. brought down on his head the wrath of the Navajo Nation Council when he proposed to reduce the council from 88 to 24 members. He argued that the council had become so bloated and bureaucratic that it was difficult to get crucial matters addressed. In a power struggle that marred his last term, Shirley brought a referendum on a reduction of the council before the Navajo people. On

December 15, 2009, the Navajo people voted to reduce the size of the council. In January 2011, the new 24-member Navajo Nation Council was seated amid accusations against almost all of the returning delegates of fraud, embezzlement, and misuse of funds. New president Ben Shelly and his vice president, Rex Lee Jim, were also accused of fraud, embezzlement, and misuse of funds. Both Shelly and Jim have offered to pay back the money they are charged with taking illegally.

Perhaps a letter written by Navajo citizens Gary Bernally and J.B. Largo Jr. indicates the depth of dissatisfaction with Navajo leaders. In their letter to the *Navajo Times*, Bernally and Largo declare, "In 2011, the Navajo Nation leadership remains as corrupt as ever. New president, vice president and the 24 delegates, every one of them are guilty of taking money or knowing of the money taken. We have delegates with alcohol problems, adulterers, thieves, wife and child beaters, etc., from the new president through the new council and local chapter officials. Greedy, hungry, powerful enough to re-establish in Navajo style the old BIA Indian educational policy 'kill the Indian, save the man.' Now it's 'kill the Dineh Indian, save myself.'"

The challenges to re-create the Navajo Nation upon the principles of cultural teaching are profound and ongoing and are happening at multiple layers in Navajo communities. The Navajo Nation and its people are always conscious that they are not only the citizens of their own nation, but they also are citizens of the United States. Like other Americans, they too have been consumed by the unfolding national events precipitated by the September 11, 2001, terrorist attacks on the World Trade Center in New York City and the Pentagon outside Washington, D.C. President George W. Bush's call to attack Iraq was answered by many Americans who joined the military, including the Navajo. Just as they have since their nation came under American rule, Navajo men and women enlisted in the U.S. military to fight in Iraq and Afghanistan. Often

(continues on page 140)

Desert Rock:
Energy Development and Resistance

In 2003, Navajo Nation president Joe Shirley Jr. unveiled his plan to establish a third coal-fired power plant in the Four Corners region in northwestern New Mexico, in the Burnham chapter. The proposed Desert Rock power plant would be a 1,500-megawatt facility built by the German company Steag Power, which was later acquired by Sithe Global Power. Historically, Navajo leaders had little control or say about how corporations conducted business on Navajo land. Desert Rock would be different, for the Navajo Nation aimed to reap the economic benefits. In addition to owning a substantial stake in the project, it was hoped that Desert Rock would put a dent in the Navajo Nation's high unemployment rate, which hovers around 48 percent. The coal-powered plant, in providing electricity to the Southwest and California, would create more than 1,600 jobs for the Navajo and bring in $50 million annually in revenues for the Navajo Nation.

Slated to be completed in 2005, many observers today have pronounced the project dead, particularly because Shirley relinquished the presidency to Ben Shelly, after serving his second term. From its inception, the proposed coal power plant met opposition from Navajo citizens who organized their communities. Navajo Nation leaders threw their support behind Desert Rock, saying that it would relieve poverty and be one of the "cleanest" coal-firing plants in the country. Meanwhile, local community members who lived near the proposed plant organized the protest against it. Community organizers charged that a third power plant in the region would significantly contribute to poor air quality and depleted water sources. In 2004 Sarah Jane White, who lived in Burnham, joined with Diné Citizens Against Ruining the Environment (CARE) to expose the dangers of the proposed power plant. White and Diné CARE formed the grassroots group Dooda

Desert Rock (No Desert Rock) and campaigned to educate the local citizens so they could make informed opinions and decisions about energy development in their communities.

In December 2006, Elouise Brown came home to discover a drilling site near her parents' home in Burnham. When a contractor appeared to monitor the site, Brown confronted him with questions until he left. With the help of her family, she erected a tent at the proposed power plant site to serve as a blockade to Sithe Global. Brown vowed that while she was alive, a third power plant would not contribute to the 57 million tons (51 million metric tons) of carbon dioxide emissions spewed annually by two aging coal-burning plants, the Four Corners Power Plant and the San Juan Generating Station, which operated within a 20-mile (32-km) radius of Brown's home.

The history of the contemporary Navajo Nation government, with the creation of the first tribal council in the 1920s, has its roots in the development of its natural resources in such a way that tribal leaders have difficulty separating the issues of sovereignty and energy development. On the one hand, male leaders have been most interested in controlling the exploitation of the rich mineral resources with an eye to bringing prosperity at costs to the environment. On the other hand, tribal leaders have always met opposition to energy development from individual Navajo and local community leaders who insist that the Navajo are quite capable of making informed decisions that will nurture a sustainable and healthy environment. Significantly, Navajo women have been at the forefront of the opposition to nationalist tribal leaders who are predominantly men. According to grassroots organizers, Navajo women follow the teachings inherent in a matricentered society in which gender is reflected in the workings of nature, earth, and human society. According to the traditional narratives, women have been primary in shaping the lifeways and ethics of the Navajo in their homeland.

(continues)

(continued)

Community organizers challenged the immense power of the Navajo Nation government, which worked in partnership with corporations and the federal and state governments to realize Desert Rock. In 2010, after relentless campaigning of New Mexico senators and leaders, the state of New Mexico rejected a proposed $85 million tax break for the project. The news has many wondering if the power plant will be built, especially as alternative energy sources are sought.

(continued from page 137)

asked why they enlist in a military that just a few generations ago was responsible for a war against them and the forced relocation to an undesirable reservation, many young Navajo say they are following a tradition set down by their grandparents who defended their country and their land. The war in Iraq is just one example of how the Diné see their dual roles as Navajo and American citizens. (They are citizens of states like New Mexico and Arizona as well.) They are proud to be Navajo who have preserved a distinct cultural heritage and proud to be Americans who are concerned about the welfare of the country.

Like other Americans, the war is just one issue they are debating, for the Nation often faces issues similar to those other U.S. citizens face. For example, Navajo citizens have debated questions about same-sex marriage, the meaning of the No Child Left Behind education policy, and the consequences of privatizing Social Security. Besides these questions, the Navajo Nation will examine taxation as a way to replace dwindling finances, consider alternative energy development, and define the role that urban Navajo—primarily those who live in Phoenix, Arizona, and Albuquerque, New Mexico—will play in the Nation. Just as the American nation is facing an economic recession, Navajo leaders are feeling the recession hit Navajoland, where unemployment hovers around 48 percent. Through all of these troubling questions about the future, of both the American nation and their own Navajo Nation, they continue to value the beliefs that saw their ancestors through good and bad times.

The Navajo way of life is shaped by federal, state, and tribal government in many ways. The People, though, take individual initiatives to claim Navajo tradition as important to their lives. Although they never forget the hardships their ancestors endured, they do not allow themselves to dwell on the past. After expressions of sadness and mourning, they shake themselves out of it and tell stories of regeneration, for it is the Navajo way to look to the future with hope for harmony and balance. Relying upon the ancient teachings embedded in Sa'ah nahagaa bi'ke'hozho, the Path of Life to Happiness and Old Age, as Navajo philosophy has been translated, the Diné strive to reclaim traditional practices that sustained their ancestors.

Chronology

1540	Spanish explorers begin to enter the Southwest.
1626	Fray Gerónimo de Zárate Salmerón makes the first Spanish reference to the "Apache Indians of Navaju."
1629	Fray Alonso de Benavides reports about the "Apache del Navajo," who live in a province beyond Spanish authority.
1659	Bernardo López de Mendízábal, the governor of New Mexico, orders raids into Navajo country for women and children, many of whom he sells into Sonora.

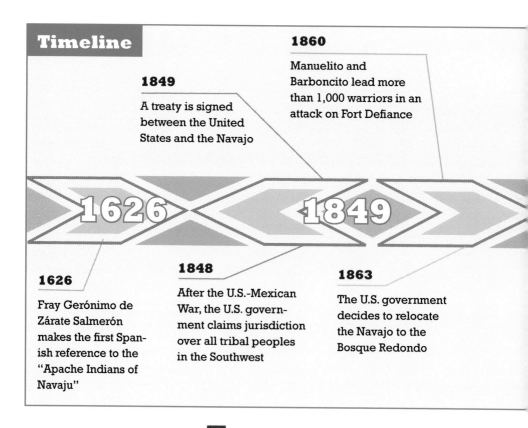

Timeline

1860
Manuelito and Barboncito lead more than 1,000 warriors in an attack on Fort Defiance

1849
A treaty is signed between the United States and the Navajo

1626

1849

1626
Fray Gerónimo de Zárate Salmerón makes the first Spanish reference to the "Apache Indians of Navaju"

1848
After the U.S.-Mexican War, the U.S. government claims jurisdiction over all tribal peoples in the Southwest

1863
The U.S. government decides to relocate the Navajo to the Bosque Redondo

1772	Navajo and Apache form an alliance and strike New Mexican settlements.
1805	Spanish troops led by Antonio Narbona kill more than 100 Navajo in a massacre at Tséyi' (Canyon de Chelly).
1820	Mexico declares independence from Spain.
1846	U.S. Army colonel Stephen Kearny claims Santa Fe, New Mexico, as a territorial capital for the United States; Navajo and U.S. officials meet at Fort Wingate, New Mexico, to establish peace.
1848	The Treaty of Guadalupe Hidalgo ends the war between the United States and Mexico. Under its terms, more than 1.2 million square miles (3.1 million square kilometers) of territory are ceded by Mexico to the United States for $15 million; the U.S. government claims jurisdiction over all tribal peoples, including the Navajo, in the Southwest.

1864

Many Navajo die during the Long Walk to the Bosque Redondo

1934–1945

The U.S. government carries out the livestock reduction program

1868 1969

1868

The Navajo and the U.S. government sign a treaty that establishes the initial boundaries of the Navajo reservation

1922

The U.S. government creates the Navajo Tribal Council

1969

The Navajo council changes the name of the Navajo Tribe to the Navajo Nation

1849	A treaty is signed between the U.S. government and the Navajo; this treaty along with one signed in 1868 are the only two of nine signed between the federal government and the Navajo that were ratified by the U.S. Senate.
1855	Manuelito is recognized as one of the leading chiefs of the Navajo tribe.
1860	Manuelito and Barboncito lead more than 1,000 warriors in an attack on Fort Defiance in New Mexico Territory.
1863	The U.S. government decides to relocate the Navajo to an area known as Bosque Redondo ("round grove," in Spanish), near Fort Sumner on the Pecos River in east-central New Mexico.
1864	Many Navajo die during the Long Walk, which was actually a series of forced marches—between 375 to 425 miles (604 to 684 kilometers)—to the Navajo reservation at Bosque Redondo.
1866	Manuelito surrenders and many Navajo leaders, including Barboncito, quickly follow suit.
1868	The Navajo and the U.S. government sign a treaty that establishes the initial boundaries of the Navajo reservation in northwestern New Mexico (about one-fourth of the tribe's traditional territory); Barboncito is the chief negotiator for the Navajo people.
1878–1886	The Navajo reservation is increased in size by five major land annexations; in the 1930s, additional lands are added to the Navajo land base.
1884	Henry Chee Dodge is named first chairman of the Navajo.
1922	The U.S. government creates the Navajo Tribal Council, which includes Chee Dodge, Charlie Mitchell, and Dugal Chee Bekiss; the men are supposed to represent their people in negotiating oil leases with the United States.
1934	The Navajo reject the Indian Reorganization Act; congressional legislation adds 243,000 acres of land to the Navajo reservation.

1934–1945   The U.S. government carries out the livestock reduction program.

1940   The Navajo pass a resolution that bans the use of peyote on reservation lands; the Native American Church, which uses the cactus in its ceremonies, holds that the resolution violates the First Amendment.

1950   Congress passes the Navajo-Hopi Long Range Rehabilitation Act, which appropriates $88 million to create an infrastructure on the Navajo and Hopi reservations. This act funds the construction of roads, schools, and hospitals. It also makes possible the development of natural resources.

1958   Congress passes a bill that allows the Navajo and Hopi tribes to sue each other to determine the rights and interests in the 1882 reservation, which is about 1.8 million acres.

1962   In *Healing v. Jones*, the U.S. District Court rules that the Hopi retain all of District 6 and "joint, undivided and equal rights" with the Navajo to the rest of the 1882 reservation.

1968   The Navajo Tribe holds a yearlong remembrance to mark the 100th anniversary of the Navajo's return from Bosque Redondo.

1969   The Navajo council officially changes the name of the Navajo Tribe to the Navajo Nation.

1974   Congress passes the Navajo-Hopi Land Settlement Act, which authorizes the partition of the Joint Use Area equally between the Navajo and Hopi tribes. Congress appropriates about $40 million for the relocation of Navajo and Hopi from lands awarded to the other side.

1996   The Hopi Tribe fashions an Accommodation Agreement that would allow Navajo who have refused to relocate to stay in their homes for 75 years under Hopi jurisdiction and with certain rules, including the number of livestock each family can have.

1998–1999	The original Treaty of 1868 is displayed at Northern Arizona University in Flagstaff, Arizona, so that Navajo may view the precious document.
2002	In an effort to return the government to a foundation based upon traditional teachings, the Navajo Nation Council enacts the Fundamental Laws of the Diné, which are signed by President Kelsey Begay.
2005	President Joe Shirley Jr. signs the Diné Natural Resources Protection Act, which bans uranium mining and processing from the Navajo Nation.
	The Bosque Redondo Memorial at Fort Sumner, New Mexico, is officially opened on June 4.
2006	Joe Shirley is elected to a second term as president of the Navajo Nation.
2011	Ben Shelly is elected president of the Navajo Nation. The 24-member Tribal Council (reduced from 88 members) takes their seats.

Glossary

Apache Indians of Navaju The earliest reference to the people who would become known as the Navajo was made by Fray Gerónimo de Zárate Salmerón in 1626. The term is said to be a Tewa word that means "large area of cultivated fields" and was applied to the ancestral Navajo to distinguish them from their Apache cousins, who did not farm to the same extent.

Asdzáá Nádleehí or Changing Woman One of the Holy People and the First Mother of the Navajo. Her name indicates the changing of the seasons. The birth of Changing Woman signaled a new era; because of her birth, a world of beauty and harmony became possible.

Bilá 'askdla' The English translation is "Five-Fingered Ones" and is another name that the Navajo call themselves. The term indicates that the Navajo are human beings.

Blessingway A central ceremony that embodies all that is significant in Navajo life and is manifested in the concept of Hózhó. The Navajo continually seek good health, peace, and prosperity throughout their lives and with their kin relations.

Bosque Redondo reservation The place where the Navajo were sent once the Americans had militarily defeated them. The reservation was intended to assimilate the Navajo captives to American ways.

Bureau of Indian Affairs (BIA) A U.S. government agency established in 1824 and assigned to the Department of the Interior in 1849. The agency was created to oversee relationships with tribes and to supervise tribes on reservations. Today, it remains involved in Indian affairs and works with tribal nations on programs such as education, health, and tribal management.

clan A unit of social organization in which an individual claims common descent through an ancestor.

code talkers A group of several hundred Navajo men who were selected by the Marine Corps during World War II to send coded messages to Pacific battlefronts. The Navajo language served as the basis for the code and was important in defeating the Japanese.

cultural pluralism   Federal Indian policy that reversed previous mandates that called for the eradication of Native cultures and languages. Instead, the new policy encouraged the preservation of cultural traditions and language.

Diné   The word that the Navajo call themselves. It means "the People."

Diné Anaa'í   This phrase translates as "Enemy Navajo" and refers to bands of Navajo who allied with the Spaniards and then the Mexicans.

Diné Bekéyah   The Navajo homeland, indicating the land between the four sacred mountains.

Dinétah   The English translation for the Navajo homeland is "among the people." Dinétah is in the San Juan River region, near Farmington, New Mexico. It is a place where the ancestors of the Diné emerged into the Glittering World, this world.

Fort Defiance   This military fort was established in 1851 in the heart of Navajo country. It became a contested site between Navajo leaders and the American military. Today, Fort Defiance, Arizona, is a Navajo community that is an important administrative center for the Navajo Nation and the Bureau of Indian Affairs.

Glittering World   The present world is called the "Glittering World." The people who became Navajo emerged into the Glittering World after a long and difficult journey.

Hero Twins   The sons of Asdzáá Nádleehí, or Changing Woman, and part of the contingent of Holy People. The Hero Twins' names are Nayee' Neizghání, or Monster Slayer, and Tóbájíshchíní, or Born for Water. Their father is Jóhonaa'éí, the Sun. The hero twins are the protectors of the land and the people.

Hózhó   A central Navajo concept that indicates the meaning of life. According to Hózhó, the Navajo continually seek good health, peace, and prosperity throughout their lives and with their kin relations.

Hwéeldi   The Navajo name for the Bosque Redondo reservation. Some say that the word is a corruption of the Spanish word for fort.

Indian Reorganization Act (IRA)   The 1934 federal law that ended the policy of allotting plots of land to individuals and provided for the political and economic development of reservation communities. The law was intended to encourage Indian self-government. The Navajo rejected the IRA because they linked it to livestock reduction.

livestock reduction   The federal policy that mandated the reduction of Navajo livestock in the 1930s and 1940s. Livestock reduction was intended to restore the land to its former condition. Ultimately, it was a failure.

Long Walk   The forced marches ranging in distance from 375 to 425 miles (604 to 684 kilometers) that Navajo prisoners endured when they were sent to the Bosque Redondo reservation from 1863 to 1868.

Manifest Destiny   According to this doctrine, white Americans were destined to spread over and claim the American continent by the will of God.

Náhookah Diné   The literal translation is "Earth Surface People" and is another name the Navajo call themselves. The phrase indicates that the People have divine origins.

Navajo in Education Sovereignty Act   In 2004, President Joe Shirley Jr. signed this legislation, which established the Navajo Board of Education and the Navajo Nation Department of Diné Education.

Radiation Exposure Compensation Act (RECA)   In 1971, Congress passed this act, which paid compassionate compensation to uranium miners who worked during the Cold War era.

Tséyi' (Canyon de Chelly)   An important site for the Navajo, the canyon is located near Chinle, Arizona. The canyon was a defensive site for the Navajo when foreign invaders attacked them.

Bibliography

Bailey, Garrick, and Roberta Glenn Bailey. *A History of the Navajos: The Reservation Years.* Santa Fe, N.M.: School of American Research, 1986.

Begay, Richard. "Tsé Bíyah 'Anii'ahí: Chaco Canyon and Its Place in Navajo History." In David Grants Nobel, ed., *In Search of Chaco: New Approaches to an Archaeological Enigma.* Santa Fe, N.M.: School of American Research Press, 2004.

Belin, Esther. *From the Belly of My Beauty: Poems.* Tucson: University of Arizona Press, 1999.

Bighorse, Tiana. *Bighorse the Warrior.* Edited by Noel Bennett. Tucson: University of Arizona Press, 1990.

Brugge, David M. *The Navajo-Hopi Land Dispute: An American Tragedy.* Albuquerque: University of New Mexico Press, 1994.

Denetdale, Jennifer Nez. *Reclaiming Diné History: The Legacies of Navajo Chief Manuelito and Juanita.* Tucson: University of Arizona Press, 2007.

Iverson, Peter. *Diné: A History of the Navajo People.* Albuquerque: University of New Mexico Press, 2002.

Jim, Rex Lee. "A Moment in My Life." In Arnold Krupat and Brian Swann, eds., *Here First: Autobiographical Essays by Native American Writers.* New York: Modern Library, 2000.

Johnson, Broderick H., ed. *Navajo Stories of the Long Walk Period.* Tsaile, Ariz.: Navajo Community College Press, 1973.

Link, Martin., ed. *The Navajo Treaty—1868: Treaty Between the United States of America and the Navajo Tribe of Indians/With a Record of the Discussions that Led to Its Signing.* Las Vegas, Nev.: K.C. Publications, 1968.

Mitchell, Frank. *Navajo Blessingway Singer: The Autobiography of Frank Mitchell, 1881–1967.* Edited by Charlotte J. Frisbie and David P. McAllester. Albuquerque: University of New Mexico Press, 1978.

Mitchell, Rose. *Tall Woman: The Life Story of Rose Mitchell, A Navajo Woman, c. 1874–1977.* Edited by Charlotte J. Frisbie. Albuquerque: University of New Mexico, Press, 2001.

Morris, Irvin. *From the Glittering World: A Navajo Story*. Norman, Okla.: University of Oklahoma Press, 1997.

O'Neill, Colleen. *Working the Navajo Way: Labor and Culture in the Twentieth Century*. Lawrence, Kan.: University Press of Kansas, 2005.

Roessel, Ruth. *Women in Navajo Society*. Rough Rock, Ariz.: Navajo Resource Center, 1981.

Spicer, Edward H. *Cycles of Conquest: The Impact of Spain, Mexico, and the United States on the Indians of the Southwest, 1533–1960*. Tucson: University of Arizona Press, 1962.

Stewart, Irene. *A Voice in Her Tribe: A Navajo Woman's Own Story*. Socorro, N.M.: Ballena Press, 1980.

Tapahonso, Luci. *Blue Horses Rush In: Poems and Stories*. Tucson: University of Arizona Press, 1997.

———. *A Breeze Swept Through*. Albuquerque: West End Press, 1987.

———. *Sáanii Dahataał: The Women Are Singing*. Tucson: University of Arizona Press, 1993.

Thompson, Gerald. *The Army and the Navajo*. Tucson: University of Arizona Press, 1976.

Tohe, Laura. *No Parole Today*. Albuquerque: West End Press, 1999.

Towner, Ronald. *Defending the Dinétah: Pueblitos in the Ancestral Navajo Heartland*. Salt Lake City: University of Utah Press, 2003.

Trafzer, Clifford E. *The Kit Carson Campaign: The Last Great Navajo War*. Norman, Okla.: University of Oklahoma Press, 1982.

Weisiger, Marsha. *Dreaming of Sheep in Navajo Country*. Seattle: University of Washington Press, 2009.

Willink, Roseann Sandoval, and Paul Zolbrod. *Weaving a World: Textiles and the Navajo Way of Seeing*. Santa Fe: Museum of New Mexico Press, 1996.

Yazzie, Ethelou. *Navajo History*. Chinle, Ariz.: Navajo Curriculum Center, Rough Rock Demonstration School, 1971.

Zolbrod, Paul. *Diné Bahane': The Navajo Creation Story*. Albuquerque: University of New Mexico Press, 1984.

Further Resources

Bruchac, Joseph. *Code Talker: A Novel About the Navajo Marines of World War Two.* New York: Speak, 2006.

———. *Navajo Long Walk.* Des Moines, Iowa: National Geographic, 2002.

Denetdale, Jennifer. *The Long Walk: The Forced Exile of the Navajo.* New York: Chelsea House Publishers, 2007.

Holm, Tom. *Code Talkers and Warriors: Native Americans and World War II.* New York: Chelsea House Publishers, 2007.

Iverson, Peter. *Diné: A History of the Navajo People.* Albuquerque: University of New Mexico Press, 2002.

Lawson, Michael L. *Little Bighorn: Winning the Battle, Losing the War.* New York: Chelsea House Publishers, 2007.

Picture Credits

Index

About the Contributors

JENNIFER DENETDALE is a Navajo of the Tł'ógi [Zia] and 'Áshįįh [Salt] clans. Originally from Tohatchi, New Mexico, she earned her Ph.D. in history from Northern Arizona University in 1999. Her research interests include Southwest Native American and Navajo history. Denetdale is the author of *Reclaiming Diné History: The Legacies of Navajo Chief Manuelito and Juanita* and Chelsea House's *The Long Walk: The Forced Navajo Exile*. She is the author of numerous articles and essays on Navajo history and culture, including women and gender.

Series editor **PAUL C. ROSIER** received his Ph.D. in American History from the University of Rochester in 1998. Dr. Rosier currently serves as Associate Professor of History at Villanova University (Villanova, Pennsylvania), where he teaches Native American History, American Environmental History, Global Environmental Justice Movements, History of American Capitalism, and World History.

In 2001, the University of Nebraska Press published his first book, *Rebirth of the Blackfeet Nation, 1912–1954*; in 2003, Greenwood Press published *Native American Issues* as part of its Contemporary Ethnic American Issues series. In 2006, he coedited an international volume called *Echoes from the Poisoned Well: Global Memories of Environmental Injustice*. Dr. Rosier has also published articles in the *American Indian Culture and Research Journal*, the *Journal of American Ethnic History*, and *The Journal of American History*. His *Journal of American History* article, entitled "They Are Ancestral Homelands: Race, Place, and Politics in Cold War Native America, 1945–1961," was selected for inclusion in *The Ten Best History Essays of 2006–2007*, published by Palgrave MacMillan in 2008; and it won the Western History Association's 2007 Arrell Gibson Award for Best Essay on the history of Native Americans. His latest book, *Serving Their Country: American Indian Politics and Patriotism in the Twentieth Century* (Harvard University Press), is winner of the 2010 Labriola Center American Indian National Book Award.